THE BIGGEST MORTGAGE FRAUD OF ALL

What, Why & The Easiest Thing To Do About It

Leon L. Morris

Published by MIFSP Publishing, a division of MIFSP, Inc.,
www.mifsp.org; publishing@myfsp.org

ISBN 9780976496755 or 0976496755
Manufactured in the United States of America
First Edition: January 2011

Table of Contents

INTRODUCTION

Many financial experts got rich over the past few years spreading the word that the best way to accumulate wealth was by using the wealth buildup in the home and by obtaining and maintaining the largest mortgage possible in order to invest money elsewhere. Some even went so far as to promote what I've referred to as the "Tag Team Mortgage Scheme" whereby a mortgage originator, under the guise of being a "mortgage planner", encouraged a homeowner to obtain a mortgage (or home equity line) and then a financial representative (planner/adviser) persuaded the homeowner to invest the proceeds with him or her. Of course, both sides of the sale were compensated. When I heard about this scheme, in 2006, I sent letters to all state regulators warning of the potential pitfalls of this scheme if there was no determination of suitability of this mortgage-investment model for the homeowners. The state of Ohio was the only state to respond that they were concerned about predatory lending and would take my suggestions into consideration as they continued to promulgate rules to better regulate the ever-evolving residential mortgage loan industry and protect Ohio's consumers.

Promoters of that business model touted that they had thousands of people from the mortgage and financial planning industry providing those types of "mortgage planning" services. However, when the housing and financial markets clasped, what do you think happened to these homeowners?

Even before 2006, in March 2005, I sent a letter to the Securities and Exchange Commission ("SEC") identifying a major flaw in the existing retail securities brokerage and investment advisory market and in the regulatory oversight and guidance that has been inadvertently, but consistently overlooked by the Commission, Self-Regulatory Organizations (SROs), broker-dealers, investment advisers, financial planners, and even academia as it relates to the blending of mortgage and investment advice. A flaw that I demonstrated by asking a rather basic question: Where should I apply my discretionary funds (a) towards prepaying my mortgage or (b) toward an investment?

I warned the SEC of the devastation Americans would face when and if the investment-mortgage advice backfired. I thought the SEC should be concerned about ill-conceived and illogical mortgage advice, and business models that resulted from an inherent undisclosed conflict of interest and the growing opportunity for fraud and misrepresentation, and the need for registered representatives and investment advisers to be better educated and sensitized to this type of blended advice as there were no statutory requirements for determining suitability when advising an investor to access home equity through a cash-out refinance, a home equity line of credit or loan, or a zero down loan for purposes of making investments or maintaining assets under management, and that there were no statutory requirements for disclosure of the differential in risks and objectives between a mortgage loan on the primary residence and the investment. However, no such rules or regulations were implemented. So, when the housing and financial markets collapsed, what do you think happened to these homeowners?

During that same time frame, I made another discovery that was even more disturbing. Banks (in all fifty states), Ginnie Mae, HUD, Freddie Mac and the U.S. Financial Literacy and Education Commission, among others all had defective rent versus buy mortgage calculators available on or through their websites that overstated the tax benefits of the mortgage interest deduction by as much as 300%. These mortgage calculators claimed to show the homeowner how much in tax savings they could expect from the mortgage under consideration. However, the faulty calculators may have created false consumer expectations of housing affordability and suitability that may have impacted mortgage defaults and foreclosures.

Grossly miscalculating and overstating the tax benefits of the mortgage interest deduction may have misled consumers into applying for and obtaining mortgages that weren't in their financial best interest. Some banks touted the benefit of the calculators in converting consumers into "interested and motivated" mortgage applicants. However, when the big mortgage interest deduction that these homebuyers were led to expect, and then counted on as the tax break that would make their dream home affordable didn't materialize, what do you think happened to these homeowners?

The report titled *The Red Report, When Banks Don't Compete – The Case of The Mortgage Calculator* identifies hundreds of banks reflecting testing of mortgage calculators found on or through websites of banks with the largest market share of deposits in the largest metropolitan areas from all fifty states. Many of these banks have since modified or removed all reference to the existence of a mortgage calculator, faulty or otherwise, but the damage has already been done and *The Red Report* may be the only document that captures their existence.

Millions of homes have been lost to foreclosure and millions more are in default. Homeowners are still trying to head off or recover from far-reaching financial devastation in the housing market and the financial markets. The calamity that I warned about through letters to state regulators, the SEC, the Board of Certified Financial Planners, the FDIC, and even the President of the United States is probably being experienced by hundreds of thousands of people at this very moment. How many homeowners were put at risk due to the fraud, misrepresentations, and disclosure failures mentioned above? How many homeowners might have avoided this financial crisis if there had been more publicized exposure of these types of deceptive business practices? How many homeowners would not now find themselves upside down in the values of their homes but for these kinds of marketing schemes that duped them into acquiring mortgages that were not in their best interest?

There is no doubt that the fraud and misrepresentations identified above could have all been avoided with greater disclosure and improved consumer knowledge. The question is: Greater disclosure of what? And improved consumer knowledge of what? Even with all of the financial calamity around us and the heightened interest in financial literacy, the answer to this question is really very simple. Once you understand this concept the way you conduct your financial life will completely change, the way you approach and manage your home financing will completely change, and the way you plan for your financial future will completely change.

The primary message in this book will come by way of a discussion of the tax benefit of the mortgage interest deduction or should I say the lack thereof. Have you every heard a mortgage referred to as "good debt" because of its tax implications? Well this book will shatter your belief in the "good debt" myth and will awaken your mind to the simplest most under disclosed and seldom discussed tax benefit available to all Americans. With required disclosure and consumer awareness of this tax benefit, not only will home buying decisions be significantly impacted, but investing, saving, retirement planning, and all major purchasing decisions will be greatly impacted as well.

If I lost you from the time I used the words "tax benefit" and since then your eyes have glazed over or you're falling into a sleep induced coma, then you are probably going to miss the major point of this book and are likely to remain vulnerable to the kinds of business practices discussed above. But if you're willing to focus more on the word "benefit" and get beyond the word "tax", then read on and you'll find out about the simplest most under disclosed and seldom discussed tax benefit available to all Americans. You'll also find out what questions to ask and how to better prepare yourself in the future when someone is giving you a marketing pitch mislabeled as financial advice. For those of you, who have already experienced financial harm due to the business practices I've described, please seek legal advice.

In Your Best Interest: If you live in a home, whether it is rented or owned, pay income taxes, sales taxes, and/or property taxes and you are concerned about the management of your money and other financial resources, this book is for you. This book is written as a small part of a much larger early warning system, a system designed specifically to help individual American consumers like you avoid and or stop being the victim of unfair, deceptive or abusive housing, tax or financial practices, and put an end to the biggest mortgage fraud of all.

In Loving Memory of:
Charles Dees
Clyde Morgan, Jr.
Nannette Smikle

Page Intentionally Left Blank

Acknowledgements

I would like to thank my wife (Allison) and children (Leena & Livingston) for their support while writing this book. I thank Everett Abney, Sr., Kenneth Clarke, Dorothy Macopson, and Willard Proctor, Jr., for their thoughtful comments on an early draft and for their encouragement. I would also like to thank Larry Fields, Steve Jones, Veronica Stokes and a host of other friends and supporters who have been kind enough to have lent me an ear over the years as I've thought and spoken almost endlessly about the essence of my message and the invisible power behind my purpose.

It is my pleasure to announce that in honor of a long-term supporter and educational consultant to the Mortgage Institute for Financial Services Professional, Inc. (MIFSP), Dr. Everett E. Abney, Sr., I've licensed to the MIFSP and made available to the readers of this book one of the tools I developed for the benefit of housing, tax and financial consumers.

The unique decision making tool (MYFSP™ C3 Exam) enables consumers, customers and clients of banks and other financial services providers to spot and stop being subjected to deceptive, fraudulent or financially manipulative sales and marketing tactics that take advantage of their lack of understanding regarding an essential housing, tax and financial issue. The tool doesn't require the consumer to try or buy any financial product or advice or under take a personal financial planning or related course of study before being able to utilize the tool effectively.

The tool is convenient and easy for consumers to use in helping them recognize a situation where their personal financial plan is built around the universal and undisputed need for housing. The tool is based upon 55 different factors but one of its primary aims is simply to bring **H**onor, **O**pportunity, **P**rofessionalism and **E**thics to the public practice of personal financial planning for the benefit of consumers so that they can make more informed decisions in their own best interest.

Page Intentionally Left Blank

Are You Financially Biased?

"The path of least resistance and least trouble is a mental rut already made. It requires troublesome work to undertake the alteration of old beliefs. Self-conceit often regards it as a sign of weakness to admit that a belief to which we have once committed ourselves is wrong. We get so identified with an idea that it is literally a "pet" notion and we rise to its defense and stop our eyes and ears to anything different."

John Dewey

A S As millions of people are losing (or have lost) their homes to foreclosure and millions of others are in default, could part of the reason for the current mortgage crisis be due to our financial bias towards something as apparently innocuous as the mortgage interest deduction. Undoubtedly, as far as the average American consumer is concerned, generally speaking, the mortgage interest deduction (MID) is and has been the most favorable annual federal tax benefit available to American homeowners for at least the last quarter century (25 years or since 1985)[1]".

Do you currently have a mortgage or have you ever had a mortgage? Do you think the mortgage interest deduction is the most favorable federal tax benefit associated with homeownership?

Here are three questions to get us started:

(1) Do you consider yourself financially competent?

(2) Are you financially biased towards the mortgage interest deduction?

(3) Do you believe banks and other institutions should be held accountable if they have engaged in unfair, deceptive and abusive financial practices that exploit your financial bias?

If you are not sure if you're biased in your view of the significance of the mortgage interest deduction, perform this objective two-minute check on the next page.

Are you, your adviser or your banker financially biased towards the Mortgage Interest Deduction?

Take This Quick Two-Minute Check

Step-One: When asked what is and/or has been the most favorable federal tax benefit available annually to American homeowners generally for at least the last quarter century (25 years or since 1985)? What tax benefit was selected? _____.

Answer:

      A) The Mortgage Interest Deduction   _____

      B) The Capital Gain Exclusion   _____

      C) Other (Not Disclosed Tax Benefit)   _____

      D) New Home Buyers Credit   _____

Step-Two: When you asked your own personal financial adviser what is and/or has been the most favorable federal tax benefit available annually to American homeowners generally for at least the last quarter century (25 years or since 1985)? What tax benefit did your adviser select? _____.

Answer:

      A) The Mortgage Interest Deduction   _____

      B) The Capital Gain Exclusion   _____

      C) Other (Not Disclosed Tax Benefit)   _____

      D) New Home Buyers Credit   _____

Step-Three: When you asked your banker (personal banker, banker financial associate, etc.) what is and/or has been the most favorable federal tax benefit available annually to American homeowners generally for at least the last quarter century (25 years or since 1985)? What tax benefit did your banker select? _____.

Answer:

        A) The Mortgage Interest Deduction   _____

        B) The Capital Gain Exclusion   _____

        C) Other (Not Disclosed Tax Benefit) _____

        D) New Home Buyers Credit   _____

Step-Four: Can you, your personal financial adviser or your banker articulate one or more reasons why the MID is the most favorable tax benefit available annually to American Homeowners?

    For example, do you "believe" some of these arguments listed?

1.   The MID encourages homeownership.

2.   The bigger the homeowner's mortgage the bigger the MID.

3.   The MID encourages people to buy the biggest house they can afford.

4.   The MID reduces the effective mortgage interest rate.

5.   The MID subsidizes homeownership for lower and middle income Americans.

Step-Five: If you are unable to articulate one or more reasons that you can support via the tax code, direct contrast with all available tax benefits or the actual experience of others, then you are in fact guess what? Biased.

Is it Ignorance or Bias?

If you couldn't compare, contrast and calculate the MID relative to all-available tax benefits, then your bias is categorical and you've moved from bias up to ignorance or more softly stated, complete unawareness.

It is often said that the American economy is based on the free enterprise system. Consumers are free to decide how to spend, save or invest their time and money. The idea is that a balance between the products and services demanded and the products and services supplied results from competition in the marketplace as various products and services are offered for sale at different price points, qualities and service levels.

In general, unless it's a hold up, no one literally holds a gun to someone's head and forces them into a transaction or exchange of either goods or services. Individuals engage in voluntary exchanges of goods and services because they believe that what they are giving up is a fair exchange or price for what they need or want.

> *"Sometimes one pays most for the things one gets for nothing."*
> Albert Einstein

Free Markets & the Information Economy

In a free market economy, the free flow of information (not that it's actually free) between people, businesses and the government promotes decision-making and action. Individuals, businesses, and the government generally, have the opportunity to make informed choices.

Making an informed choice doesn't mean that the right choice or even the best possible choice is always made, only that the individual decision maker is generally able to pursue their lives, while exercising their freedom to choose what they believe will make them satisfied or happy. You like others have probably said, and some would argue, that our economy is in part an information economy. Knowledge is considered the primary raw material and source of value. In such an economy, information like other goods and services is produced and distributed in the marketplace.

In a free-market, it is theorized that those who have the information are free to make an exchange with those who don't. Again, the reason why the exchange takes place is that those involved believe the information has value. This is one reason why it is particularly important that we are able to identify and distinguish between those who make us aware of relevant and timely information and those who, among other things, do the opposite.

This difference in haves and have-nots of information creates numerous possibilities. According to www.BusinessDictionay.com, information in general is data that has been (1) verified to be accurate and timely, (2) is specific and organized for a purpose, (3) is presented within a context that gives it meaning and relevance, and which (4) leads to the increase in understanding and decrease in uncertainty. The value of information lies solely in its ability to affect behavior, decision, or outcome. A piece of information is considered valueless if, after receiving it, things remain unchanged.

The MID Has Value

The MID has value even before we get into any numbers simply because it has a historically documented and proven ability to not only impact behavior, but also decisions and outcomes. However, what if you discovered that the level of information you have regarding the mortgage interest deduction differed greatly from the level of information known by banks, your financial adviser or the government?

One Reason We May Have Developed a Bias Towards the Mortgage Interest Deduction

Our bias toward the mortgage interest deduction may be thanks in part to the Tax Reform Act of 1986, which allowed taxpayers to deduct the interest for consumer loans only if the loan is secured by the home. The result was that the benefits of the mortgage interest deduction on a home loan were used to sell the idea for everything from consolidating debt, to buying cars, to getting a larger home and/or a larger home loan, to finding funds for investing. Sadly, the benefits of the mortgage interest deduction were promoted with little regard to how it really affects taxes, its true impact on the consumer's earnings or the continuing need to earn. We were led to see as much or more value in this remaining interest deduction than in the value of the build up of home equity that was leading us toward a paid for home.

To help move our thoughts in that direction some (people with a vested interest in our thinking this way) argued that if money was sitting in the equity of the consumer's home, it was not at work, that it was a wasted asset. However, we should realize that it's quite the opposite. That money is working. It's working to reduce the amount of other money that must be at work. It's working to provide a tax-free way to save. It's working to reduce the amount of income that must be produced. It's working to reduce the amount of money needed at retirement. And it's working to protect the home from risks associated with negative changes to the consumer's overall financial situation.

Another Reason We May Have Developed a Bias Towards the Mortgage Interest Deduction

When it comes to calculating the marginal tax savings from the mortgage interest deduction, most people who dispense financial advice ("experts") fail to calculate it properly. Quite simply, they fail to realize that mortgage interest may not result in any tax savings if itemized deductions do not exceed the standard deduction set by tax filing status, and that it is only the amount by which the itemized deductions exceed the standard deduction that the taxpayer receives any tax savings. However, these experts seem to overlook that.

According to IRS data[2], only 25.4% of all individual tax returns filed in 2008 included a mortgage interest deduction. In other words, taxpayers should be more concerned with tax laws that propose to change the amount of the standard deduction than with those that propose to eliminate the mortgage interest deduction.

Couple the mistakes of some experts with the willful exploitation by other trusted sources mentioned earlier, and then you'll see another reason that we may have developed a bias towards the mortgage interest deduction.

The Information Gap

Wouldn't you agree that this difference in information levels could open up a type of Pandora's box to the potential for deception, fraud, and abusive, unfair and uneconomical business practices?

This difference in information (information asymmetry) creates market inefficiencies because some market participants like the banks and the government have better and more relevant information than most housing, tax and financial consumers as it relates to aggregated personal housing, tax and financial decision making.

What would you do if you discovered that the dollar value of the tax break you believed you would get from the mortgage interest deduction turned out to be untrue, a falsehood, a lie? What if you were depending on the value of this "tax break" to make housing (the mortgage) affordable?

The Red Report, When Banks Don't Compete – The Case of The Mortgage Calculator, is a national study of the online mortgage marketing practices of FDIC insured banks with a 1% or greater market share of bank deposits in the largest Metropolitan Area in every state of he Union. The study specifically tested the accuracy of Rent v. Buy (RvB) and Save In tax (SiTx) financial calculators made available online. Three model client scenarios, Section 5 of the Federal Trade Commission Act and the Herfindahl-Hirschman Index of market concentration served as benchmarks. All calculators tested proved defective in that they overstated the tax benefits of the mortgage interest deduction by as much as 300%. Had the users of these faulty calculators been aware of that discrepancy, do you think it would have altered their behavior?

Mortgage Calculators Have Value

Just like the mortgage interest deduction, mortgage calculators, faulty or not, have a value simply because they have the ability to impact behavior, a decision or an outcome as the providers of those calculators found out.

In the case of those who used a faulty mortgage calculator, it is possible that a decision based on the belief of an inflated mortgage interest deduction could have resulted in a negative financial impact. Is that unfair? Is that deceptive? Is that abusive?

Those who sold or benefited from the consumers' use of faulty mortgage calculators made "extraordinary" profits so it may seem reasonable to expect that those individual companies that made and distributed the calculators should be held accountable, as should those who used them strategically to promote their products and services at the expense of the user.

This is where the magical world of loopholes and information becomes of great value to those who have the information, and it becomes even more costly for those who can't afford to pay for the information or don't have sufficient information, awareness, knowledge, intelligence, or the inclination to ask. Now let's examine the flip side of a mortgage.

The Simplest, Undervalued, and Most Completely Ignored Tax Benefit of True Homeownership

"Any intelligent fool can make things bigger and more complex... It takes a touch of genius - and a lot of courage to move in the opposite direction."
Albert Einstein

In a white paper called "Analysis of the Advantages in Prepaying the Mortgage," I perform an analysis that documents the best tax benefit of true homeownership and demonstrates the need for residential mortgage planning. The paper notes that "consumers either commonly bypass, or are being diverted from the opportunity to achieve financial independence by ignoring the lowest risk, no cost alternative to investing; namely, paying down or off the mortgage. The paper also explains the basis of the Mortgage Portfolio Theory, promoted by the Mortgage Institute for Financial Service Professionals, Inc. (MIFSP), which recognizes that "a mortgage free home is a defensive investment portfolio position, an excellent hedge against inflation and a safe-harbor in an investment market down turn especially where there is an unexpected loss of income."

I chose to perform this analysis because I could not find any evidence where financial planning associations or other financial professionals had offered consumers a clear and proper answer to the question of whether to use discretionary funds to invest or pay down the mortgage. In other analyses, I've seen where comparisons were made between the rate of return of an investment and mortgage prepayment choices, but what seems to be overlooked is the fact that the mortgage must be paid. Consideration is not given to the need to continue servicing the debt when funds are diverted elsewhere. It's not an apples to apples comparison because the mortgage is a contractual obligation to pay, not a discretionary debt, and the longer it takes to pay off the mortgage the more it costs regardless of tax deductibility factors. Consequently, the consumer had to keep working to pay the mortgage while waiting for the investment to grow.

During my analysis, I realized the question is not whether or not to prepay the mortgage because the answer to this question will most likely always be in favor of prepaying the mortgage if the analysis is performed correctly. Given the tradeoffs, it would be hard for any investment to beat the wide-ranging benefits and extremely low risk of living in a debt free home. Therefore, the real question is: How do you go about structuring a plan to prepay your mortgage that is right for you given your particular situation? I then formulated a calculation to use in structuring an individual plan for this purpose. It's called the Comparable Equivalent Yield (CEY). Consequently, my analyses caused me to take a deeper look into the question of the tax benefits of having a mortgage. What I learned made me a devout enthusiast of the simplest, undervalued, and most completely ignored tax benefit of true homeownership.

Imputed Rental Value (IRV)

The following two paragraphs were taken from *The Red Report*:

> In an all cash home purchase, even though the purchaser does not receive tax savings from the mortgage interest deduction, a proper Rent versus Buy analysis should consider the savings related to (1) not paying rent and (2) no taxation on the "fair rental price" or the net rental value of the home. The tax benefit of not being taxed on the "fair rental price" of the home can be calculated and should be considered along with any other identified and related costs or benefits by anyone exploring the costs and benefits (contrasting) of renting versus buying a home.

> While the financial and tax benefits of owning a home/house without a mortgage can be easily determined, it is important to note neither the financial benefits nor the tax benefit(s) of not having a mortgage is neither considered, nor weighed in the calculation, determination, or illustration of either the financial or tax benefits of renting versus buying a home by the calculators tested.

Here when I use the term "imputed rental value", it's synonymous with the terms "fair rental price" or "estimated rental value" minus allowable expenses and/or "net rental value." In other words, it's the amount of rent a person who is not related to you would be willing to pay to live in your house minus allowable expenses. The financial benefit of living in a completely paid for home is that this store of value is excluded from an individual's taxable or adjusted gross income (AGI) and as the individual's equity in the home grows (or as rents equal, exceed and/or rise as fast or faster than allowable expenses), so does the tax-free benefit associated with the Fair Rental Price minus expenses (net rental value). So for those looking for a tax-free haven in which to accumulate wealth, paying for your home is it. There are also estate planning benefits associated with passing on a paid for home. Ask your tax advisor about that. Okay. Now you know the simplest, undervalued, and most completely ignored tax benefit associated with true homeownership.

Banks and others generally fail to disclose, illustrate, or otherwise explain the availability or significance of the imputed rental value anytime they mention the mortgage interest deduction and that creates the impression that the most significant tax benefit available annually to the homeowners is the mortgage interest deduction. However, generally, in order to receive any tax benefit associated with the mortgage interest deduction a homeowner has to have a qualified home, meaning that their house, condominium, cooperative, mobile home, house trailer, boat, or similar property must have sleeping, cooking, and toilet facilities, whereas a homeowner can realize a tax benefit associated with the imputed rental value without meeting any such requirements. Has this disclosure ever been made to you? No? Does knowing that change your bias towards the mortgage interest deduction in any away? If so, then for you banks have been withholding behavior and decision-making information before, during and after origination of a mortgage that puts you in financial harms way and which can cause substantial financial damage.

There are even more requirements that must be met in order to receive the mortgage interest deduction.

Filing Requirements to Receive the Mortgage Interest Deduction

All the tax benefits associated with the imputed rental value are available to all owner occupied homeowners while the tax benefits associated with the mortgage interest deduction are not. For example, in order to receive any tax benefit associated with the mortgage interest deduction, a homeowner must agree to sign an instrument such as a mortgage or deed of trust that makes their ownership in the home security for payment of a debt, while a homeowner can realize a tax benefit associated with the imputed rental value without using their home for security for any debt. Also, a homeowner must agree that in case of default the home could satisfy the debt in order to qualify for the mortgage interest deduction. Whereas a homeowner can realize a tax benefit associated with the imputed rental value without being required to secure any debt with their home. Moreover, the instrument used has to be recorded or otherwise perfected under applicable state or local law in order to receive the benefit under the mortgage interest deduction. A homeowner can realize a tax benefit associated with the imputed rental value without satisfying any of these three requirements.

	MID	**IRV**
Tax benefit available to all homeowners?	No	Yes
Homeowner must sign an instrument?	Yes	No
Home must be security for debt in case of default?	Yes	No
Mortgage/Deed Instrument must be recorded?	Yes	No

Requirements regarding Tax Returns

A homeowner's itemized deductions must exceed the standard deduction for their filing status in order to receive the mortgage interest deduction, while homeowners can realize a tax benefit associated with the imputed rental value whether or not their itemized deductions exceed the standard deduction. Also, to receive a tax benefit from the mortgage interest deduction, a homeowner has to annually file Internal Revenue Service (IRS) long Form 1040 and a Schedule A, while a homeowner can realize a tax benefit associated with the imputed rental value even if they file IRS Form 1040EZ, 1040A or 1040 and no Schedule A or no income tax return at all.

What follows are other limitations surrounding the mortgage interest deduction:

- o The deductibility of qualified mortgage insurance is limited by a homeowner's filing status and adjusted gross income (for example the deductibility is limited when adjusted gross income reaches $100,000 if married filing jointly (MFJ) or $50,000 if single or married filing separately, and is eliminated completely when AGI exceeds $109,000 MFJ or $54,500 otherwise), while there are no income or filing status limitations on the availability of any tax benefit associated with the Imputed Rental Value.

o There are limits on the deductibility of qualified home mortgage interest expense in that it cannot exceed one million dollars $1,000,000 if married filing jointly (MFJ) or $500,000 if single or married filing separately, while there is no limit to the availability of any tax benefit associated with the imputed rental value.

o There are limits on the deductibility of interest related to home equity debt in that it cannot exceed one hundred thousand dollars $100,000 if married filing jointly (MFJ) or $50,000 if single or married filing separately, while there is no mortgage debt that automatically limits the availability of any tax benefit associated with the imputed rental value.

o In general, in order to receive any tax benefit associated with the mortgage interest deduction, a homeowner has to have a qualified debt that they paid interest on in the tax year that they hope to receive a mortgage interest deduction related benefit from, whereas a homeowner can realize a tax benefit associated

with the imputed rental value whether or not they pay
any interest expenses in a particular tax year or not.

o   A homeowner has to maintain records and be ready to
    substantiate all mortgage interest deduction related items,
    whereas a homeowner can realize a tax benefits associated with
    the imputed rental value without substantiating the amount of
    any benefit.

o   A homeowner can have the amount of their mortgage interest
    deduction related items subject to audit by the Internal
    Revenue Service, whereas a homeowner can realize a tax
    benefits associated with the imputed rental value and never
    have it audited by the IRS.

o   A homeowner can have the amount of their mortgage interest
    deduction related items adjusted by the Internal Revenue
    Service, whereas a homeowner can realize tax benefits
    associated with the imputed rental value and never have it
    adjusted by the IRS.

So, now that I've introduced or re-introduced you to the concept of
imputed rental value, I'll ask the question again: Have you been
financially biased towards the mortgage interest deduction? Have you
previously recognized that you held this bias at all? Have you realized
how your financial bias could be used against you in making mortgage
and investment decisions? Have you ever considered that awareness of

the imputed rental value, or value of a mortgage free home, could influence your mortgage and investment decisions? Have you ever considered that without disclosure of the imputed rental value of homeownership you were being denied material information that may have impacted your mortgage and/or investment decisions? Have you ever considered that by feeding your financial bias towards the mortgage interest deduction you have been led into possibly missing out on the simplest, undervalued, and most completely ignored tax benefit of true homeownership?

Before anyone read *The Red Report*, I intended there to be an implied message that the real problem went far beyond the mortgage calculators, being that calculators are used to solve problems; they are usually not the problem or even part of the problem, hence the subtitle "when banks don't compete – the case of the mortgage calculator". After reading *The Red Report*, one would be aware of a laundry list of problems (from a-z) with the calculators, but the single biggest problem mentioned in the conclusion is directly related to competition and the fact that "There is a lack of objective mortgage financial advice in the marketplace[3]". The bigger problem which wasn't being addressed or solved was that banks don't compete in the provision of objective mortgage financial advice. Banks uniformly fail to mention the IRV and that's a practice that's likely to continue to cause substantial financial harm to consumers, but is this practice unfair, deceptive and/or abusive?

RECOGNIZABLE & AVOIDABLE PRACTICES

Notes:

Unfair Practices

"A man's ethical behavior should be based effectually on sympathy, education, and social ties; no religious basis is necessary. Man would indeed be in a poor way if he had to be restrained by fear of punishment and hope of reward after death."
Albert Einstein

A S demonstrated by the faulty mortgage calculators previously discussed, a consumer's inability to differentiate between marketing material and educational or informational material can lead to financial harm, but is the provision of those calculators unlawful? Section 1031 of the new *Dodd-Frank Wall Street Reform and Consumer Protection Act* refers to the specific authority the new Bureau of Consumer Protection has to prohibit unfair, deceptive, or abusive acts or practices and that the Bureau can prescribe rules identifying what unfair, deceptive or abusive acts or practices are unlawful. For those who are unfamiliar with this Act, the stated aim given in the preamble to the act is:

> "To promote the financial stability of the United States by improving accountability and transparency in the financial system, to end "too big to fail", to protect the

American taxpayer by ending bailouts, to protect
consumers from abusive financial services practices,
and for other purposes."

One of things American families, homeowners, prospective

homeowners, investors, taxpayers and financial services consumers

need to be aware of is that in order for an act or practice to be declared

unlawful it can not simply be deceptive, unfair or abusive as a

consumer is likely to use and understand those words. For example, a

consumer might think that a deceptive act or practice that misleads and

causes financial harm to consumers should be declared unlawful.

The reality is that before an act or practice can be declared unlawful it

has to meet certain conditions. In order to develop a working

familiarity with the applicable actual and practical aspects of

(examining) consumer protection relative to the real world of financial

services it is important that housing, tax and financial services

consumers be aware of these additional hoops or conditions that must

be satisfied otherwise you might as well call them loopholes.

In support of an examination and demonstration of just how common

it is for the average American to be subjected to unfair, deceptive and

abusive financial services practices, it is necessary to understand how

those terms are actually defined in the law.

Long before the establishment of the new Bureau of Consumer

Protection, there has been in existence a Federal Agency whose

primary aim has been the prevention of business practices that are

anticompetitive, deceptive or unfair to consumers. This agency's mission is to enhance informed consumer choice and public understanding of the competitive process without standing in the way of legitimate business activity. The agency is better known as the Federal Trade Commission (FTC) and it has been around since 1913.

The Standard Established By the Federal Trade Commission

According to the FTC, an act or practice may be found to be *unfair* where it "causes or is likely to cause substantial injury to consumers which is not reasonably avoidable by consumers themselves and not outweighed by countervailing benefits to consumers or to competition." This standard was first issued as a policy by the FTC and later codified into the FTC Act as 15 U.S.C. § 45(n).

In summary, the three essential conditions for an act or practice to be considered unfair are:

1. Does or is the omission, act, or practice likely to cause substantial injury to consumers?
2. Can consumers reasonably avoid the omission, act, or practice?
3. Does the omission, act, or practice produce countervailing benefits for consumers or competition?

Let's explore each of these essential conditions in more detail from a layman's perspective, being that nothing in this book should be considered to be legal advice.

Condition 1: Does or is the Omission, Act, or Practice Likely to Cause Substantial Injury to Consumers?

The harm that can be caused by, or likely to continue to be caused by, faulty mortgage calculators, as stated in *The Red Report,* is not trivial, or emotional, but it is and can continue to cause substantial financial injury to consumers all across the country.

> Every three months, 250,000 new families enter into foreclosure (Source: Mortgage Bankers Association)

The individuals and families harmed by these faulty calculators include:

- Consumers who are trying to weigh the cost of buying a home versus renting a home.

- Consumers who are unable to pay the purchase price of a home in full on closing day.

- Consumers who seek mortgage financing information from a bank believed to be a trusted, credible and/or reliable source of information.

- Consumers who are led to believe that the single largest or most significant tax benefit available annually to homeowners is the morgage interest deduction.

- Consumers who are led to believe that there are no tax benefits or consequences associated with renting a home.

- And consumers who believed that "Rent v. Buy" or "Save in Tax" mortgage calculators work correctly, among others.

Being that most consumers perceive banks as trustworthy, credible and reliable sources of mortgage finance information, they will most likely believe that information received through bank websites is also trustworthy, credible, and reliable. However, if consumers were counting on the tax savings as computed by these calculators to ease the financial burden of the mortgage and make it affordable, then the consumer's determination of mortgage affordability was highly compromised. In cases like that, are the faulty mortgage calculators likely to cause substantial injury to those consumers? Probably yes.

The Red Report says it best:

> As a consequence of using Rent v. Buy and Save In Tax mortgage calculators, unsuspecting consumers are likely being led into mortgage transactions expecting to enjoy mortgage related tax savings that won't occur and/or believing that a mortgage is a tax wise step, while not being made aware of the tax benefit of a (optimal) mortgage or a mortgage free home. Someone making a rent versus buy decision counting on the overstated tax benefit of the mortgage interest deduction could be misled from the outset. This wrong signal could result in financial harm to consumers.

Condition 2: Can Consumers Reasonably Avoid The Omission, Act, or Practices?

In determining whether or not the provision of faulty mortgage calculators constitutes an omission, act or practice that consumers could reasonably avoid, let's consider this statement from the FTC:

> "A practice is not considered unfair if consumers may reasonably avoid injury. Consumers cannot reasonably avoid injury from an act or practice if it interferes with their ability to effectively make decisions. Withholding material price information until after the consumer has committed to purchase the product or service would be an example of preventing a consumer from making an informed decision. A practice may also be unfair where consumers are subject to undue influence or are coerced into purchasing unwanted products or services.
>
> The Agencies will not second- guess the wisdom of particular consumer decisions. Instead, the Agencies will consider whether a bank's behavior unreasonably creates or takes advantage of an obstacle to the free exercise of consumer decision-making."
>
> *Unfair or Deceptive Acts or Practices: State Chartered Banks*, page 3, Board of Governors of the Federal Reserve, Federal Deposit Insurance Corporation (March 11, 2004).

Banks spend a great deal of money annually on promotional advertising in order to garner and maintain the trust of the consuming public. Therefore, if these highly regarded entities led consumers to obtain a mortgage using the guise of a grossly exaggerated tax deduction, would you consider that coercion? Would the fact that this exaggerated tax deduction was the only tax benefit of homeownership mentioned by this trusted entity further coerce the consumer into obtaining a mortgage rather than seeking some other tax benefit of homeownership? Should a consumer be expected to avoid and distrust information provided through their trusted bank?

97% Of All Mortgages are Institutional Mortgages not seller provided financing in the USA from 2000-1010. Source: Federal Reserve Board Data

---

The study documented in *The Red Report* shows that banks across America provide access to faulty mortgage calculators that illustrate an annual percentage rate (APR) that takes into account the expected benefit from the mortgage interest deduction thereby distorting mortgage costs. Therefore, by relying on these faulty calculators, millions of consumers could be misled as to what the actual APR on their mortgage will be.

Condition 3: Does the Omission, Act or Practice Produce Countervailing Benefits For Consumers or Competition?

To be injurious in its net effects " the injury must not be outweighed by any offsetting consumer or competitive benefits that are also produced by the act or practice. Offsetting benefits may include lower prices or a wider availability of products and services." *Unfair or Deceptive Acts or Practices: State Chartered Banks*, page 3, Board of Governors of the Federal Reserve, Federal Deposit Insurance Corporation (March 11, 2004). The FTC goes on to explain that "[c]osts that would be incurred for remedies or measures to prevent the injury are also taken into account in determining whether an act or practice is unfair. In this case, these costs may include the costs to the bank in taking preventive measures and the costs to society as a whole of any increased burden and similar matters." *Id.*

The Red Report identifies hundreds of banks and other entities providing access to faulty mortgage calculators, thus the subtitle "when banks don't compete." Therefore, they were obviously not competing to provide objective mortgage financial information or advice. And to the extent that any of the billions of dollars required for the bank bailout or the millions of dollars lost to foreclosure are due in any part to the misinformation spread by faulty mortgage calculators, I am at a loss in trying to identify any countervailing benefit for consumers or competition.

In addition to the three conditions identified, the FTC has indicated that public policy is also considered. The FTC describes the public policy considerations as follows:

> Public policy, as established by statute, regulation, or judicial decisions may be considered with all other evidence in determining whether an act or practice is unfair. For example, the fact that a particular lending practice violates a state law or a banking regulation may be considered as evidence in determining whether the act or practice is unfair. Conversely, the fact that a particular practice is affirmatively allowed by statute may be considered as evidence that the practice is not unfair. Public policy considerations by themselves, however, will not serve as the primary basis for determining that an act or practice is unfair.
>
> *Unfair or Deceptive Acts or Practices: State Chartered Banks*, page 3, Board of Governors of the Federal Reserve, Federal Deposit Insurance Corporation (March 11, 2004)

Unfair Practices Conclusion

The larger unfair banking practice goes beyond creating, placing and otherwise providing access to faulty mortgage calculators on or through websites. What you should recognize by now is that the bigger unfair banking practice is that banks have perpetually failed to disclose, discuss, clarify, illustrate, or otherwise explain, compare, contrast or compute the availability or significance of the imputed rental value or amount, which is a tax benefit that is easier to qualify for, more widely available, and significantly less costly for owner occupied property owners than the mortgage interest deduction. Rather than exploiting the financial bias held by most consumers towards the mortgage interest deduction, the financial benefit of the imputed rental value should be disclosed anytime the mortgage interest deduction is mentioned. When it's not disclosed before a mortgage is sold, millions of consumers are prevented from making an informed decision because they are being denied material information that results in incomplete cost information. The faulty mortgage calculators illustrate an annual percentage rate that takes into account an over inflated mortgage interest deduction, which thereby distorts mortgage costs. The mortgage ends up costing far more than the consumer was led to believe it would, which means that banks engage in unfair practices (business practices) that go beyond being likely to cause substantial financial injury to consumers by actually causing substantial financial injury to consumers.

Many of those seeking information are first time homebuyers, which makes them likely to be less savvy when it comes to analyzing the financial benefits of homeownership. Instead of providing reasonably sound financial information, these institutions capitalize on their business position and perpetuate financial myths (homeownership, mortgage finance and federal tax myths).

NOTES:

Deceptive Practices

"When the eyes say one thing and the tongue another, the practiced person relies on the language of the first."
- Ralph Waldo Emerson -

T he fact that an act or practice is unfair doesn't automatically mean that it is also deceptive. Although that could be the case, it is important to note that a deceptive act or practice is broadened to include a representation and that representation or presentation of fact maybe by words (explicit) or by conduct (implicit).

The FTC Set the Standard Adopted By the Federal Reserve, the FDIC & Others

An act or practice is "deceptive" if there is a representation, omission or practice that (1) misleads or is likely to mislead consumers; (2) where the consumer's interpretation of the representation, omission, or practice is reasonable under the circumstances; and (3) the representation, omission, or practice is material." *Unfair or Deceptive Acts or Practices: State Chartered Banks*, Board of Governors of the Federal Reserve, Federal Deposit Insurance Corporation (March 11, 2004).

A deceptive act or practice is further described as follows:

> "Deception is not limited to situations in which a consumer
> has already been misled. Instead, an act or practice may be
> found to be deceptive if it is likely to mislead consumers. A
> representation may be in the form of express or implied claims
> or promises and may be written or oral. Omission of
> information may be deceptive if disclosure of the omitted
> information is necessary to prevent a consumer from being
> misled." *Unfair or Deceptive Acts or Practices: State Chartered Banks*,
> Pg 4, Board of Governors of the Federal Reserve, Federal
> Deposit Insurance Corporation (March 11, 2004)

As it relates to the acts and practices of banks across America, which
were discussed in Units 1 and 2, do they meet the three-part definition
of deceptive? Let's examine each of the three parts.

Part 1. Are the banks representations, omissions and practices deceptive?

> "In determining whether an individual statement,
> representation, or omission is misleading, the statement,
> representation, or omission will not be evaluated in isolation.
> The Agencies will evaluate it in the context of the entire
> advertisement, transaction, or course of dealing to determine
> whether it constitutes deception. Acts or practices that have
> the potential to be deceptive include: making misleading cost
> or price claims; using bait-and-switch techniques; offering to
> provide a product or service that is not in fact available;
> omitting material limitations or conditions from an offer;
> selling a product unfit for the purposes for which it is sold; and
> failing to provide promised services." *Unfair or Deceptive Acts or
> Practices: State Chartered Banks*, Pg 4, Board of Governors of the
> Federal Reserve, Federal Deposit Insurance Corporation
> (March 11, 2004)

Banks across America have targeted their representations towards some of the most vulnerable consumers during a time when they are most vulnerable.

And the representations and marketing practices that are in question include:

- ❑ Promoting or otherwise perpetuating the belief that the mortgage interest deduction is the single largest or most significant tax benefit available annually to American homeowners.

- ❑ Giving potential mortgagors a one-sided view of the tax benefits of homeownership by failing to disclose that a paid for home also has tax benefits.

- ❑ Leading consumers to use faulty "Rent v. Buy" mortgage calculators.

- ❑ Profiting from providing (targeted) consumers access to faulty "Rent v. Buy" mortgage calculators that, among other things, grossly overstate the benefits of the mortgage interest deduction.

- ❑ Leading consumers to draw certain conclusions regarding mortgage affordability based on the benefits of tax savings associated with the mortgage interest deduction as determined by a faulty mortgage calculator.

❑ Leading consumers to draw certain conclusions regarding mortgage suitability based on the benefits of tax savings associated with the mortgage interest deduction as determined by a faulty mortgage calculator.

So what was omitted? In the quest to sell a mortgage, listed below are specific examples of omitted material information that misleads consumers and perpetuates the housing, tax and financial myth that the mortgage interest deduction is the most advantageous or most significant tax benefit available to American homeowners on an annual basis. (Some of these I may have already mentioned in previous sections, but they are worth repeating.)

Banks have regularly:

1. Omitted illustrating, educating or otherwise telling consumers about the availability or significance of the other tax benefit associated with homeownership, the Imputed Rental Value.

2. Omitted telling consumers that "Rent V. Buy" and Save in Tax mortgage calculators, that banks across America have provided access to, don't disclose, illustrate, or otherwise explain the availability or significance of the Imputed Rental Value as a tax benefit of homeownership.

3. Omitted disclosing, illustrating, or otherwise explaining the availability or significance of the imputed rental value anytime they mention the mortgage interest deduction; thus, creating the impression that the most significant tax benefit available annually to the homeowners is the mortgage interest deduction.

4. Omitted disclosing to consumers that the tax benefits associated with the imputed rental value are <u>available to all</u> owner occupied homeowners while the tax benefits associated with the mortgage interest deduction are not.

5. Omitted disclosing, illustrating, or otherwise explaining to consumers that the tax benefits associated with the imputed rental value are available to consumers whether they rent, finance or own their own home while the tax benefits associated with the mortgage interest deduction are not.

6. Omitted disclosing, illustrating, or otherwise explaining to consumers that in general a homeowner's itemized deductions must exceed the standard deduction for their filing status in order to benefit from the mortgage interest deduction, while homeowners can realize a tax benefit associated with the imputed rental value whether or not their itemized deductions exceed the standard deduction.

7. Omitted disclosing, illustrating, or otherwise explaining to consumers that the mortgage interest deduction can substantially increase the cost of homeownership whereas consumers can benefit from the imputed rental value without incurring any additional costs of homeownership.

8. Omitted disclosing, illustrating, or otherwise explaining to consumers that the mortgage interest deduction cannot only increase the costs of homeownership, but that it also negatively impacts or otherwise reduces the tax benefits associated with the imputed rental value while failing to disclose that the imputed rental value has no similar negative and automatic impact on those individuals who benefit from the mortgage interest deduction.

9. Omitted disclosing, illustrating, or otherwise explaining to consumers that, all else being equal, the tax benefits associated with the mortgage interest deduction are generally reduced annually over the life of a typical fixed rate mortgage and end up being worthless, whereas as the tax benefits associated with the imputed rental value for that same individual rises.

10. Omitted disclosing, illustrating, or otherwise explaining to consumers that as a tax benefit, the mortgage interest deduction is not as widely available, as cheap, as easy to

qualify for, as free of restrictions, as beneficial, (durable, long lasting) or enduring a tax benefit as the imputed rental value

Do you think that if it were not for those representations and omissions, your bias towards the mortgage interest deduction would have changed and/or your mortgage and investment decisions would have been different?

Part 2. Were the Consumer's Interpretation of the Bank's Representations, Omissions, and Practices Reasonable Under the Circumstances?

"The act or practice must be considered from the perspective of the reasonable consumer. In determining whether an act or practice is misleading, the consumer's interpretation of or reaction to the representation, omission, or practice must be reasonable under the circumstances. The test is whether the consumer's expectations or interpretation are reasonable in light of the claims made. When representations or marketing practices are targeted to a specific audience, such as the elderly or the financially unsophisticated, the standard is based upon the effects of the act or practice on a reasonable member of that group."

"In evaluating whether a representation, omission or practice is deceptive, the Agencies will look at the entire advertisement, transaction, or course of dealing to determine how a reasonable consumer would respond. Written disclosures may be insufficient to correct a misleading statement or representation, particularly where the consumer is directed away from qualifying limitations in the text or is counseled that reading the disclosures is unnecessary. Likewise, oral disclosures or fine print may be insufficient to cure a misleading headline or prominent written representation." *Unfair or Deceptive Acts or Practices: State Chartered Banks*, Pg 4&5, Board of Governors of the Federal Reserve, Federal Deposit Insurance Corporation (March 11, 2004)

Let's make this short. I believe the consumers' interpretation of the accuracy and completeness of the banks' representations are very reasonable under the circumstances, being that banks across the country:

✓ Represent, market, or otherwise imply, among other things, that they are sound and trustworthy sources of mortgage finance information.

✓ Represent, market, or otherwise imply that they are proficient sources of mortgage finance information.

✓ Represent, market, or otherwise imply that they are credible and reliable sources of mortgage finance information.

Part 3. Are the Bank's Representations, Omissions and Practices Material?

According to the Joint Statement of the banking regulators:

> "A representation, omission, or practice is material if it is likely to affect a consumer's decision regarding a product or service. In general, information about costs, benefits, or restrictions on the use or availability of a product or service is material. When express claims are made with respect to a financial product or service, the claims will be presumed to be material. Similarly, the materiality of an implied claim will be presumed when it is demonstrated that the institution intended that the consumer draw certain conclusions based upon the claim.
>
> Claims made with the knowledge that they are false will also be presumed to be material. Omissions will be presumed to be material when the financial institution knew or should have

known that the consumer needed the omitted information to evaluate the product or service." *Unfair or Deceptive Acts or Practices: State Chartered Banks*, Pg 5, Board of Governors of the Federal Reserve, Federal Deposit Insurance Corporation (March 11, 2004)

During the study that lead to *The Red Report*, it was discovered that some banks touted the fact the these types of mortgage calculators I've been discussing not only helped them capture prospects, but helped convert consumers into "interested and motivated" mortgage applicants. This indicates an awareness of the consumer and the marketing uses of these calculators and the material impact they had on consumer mortgage decisions.

What do you think? Are these deceptive practices or not? Given what you know thus far, can we rightfully conclude that banks across America have for years done any or all of the following?

☐ Regularly encouraged consumers to crunch the numbers and obtain a loan after making "faulty" mortgage calculators available that among other things overstate the benefits from the mortgage interest deduction.

☐ Perpetuated the belief that the mortgage interest deduction is the most significant tax benefit available annually to homeowners.

☐ Made "representations, omissions and engaged in practices" that they knew or should have known affected and are likely to continue to affect a consumer's decision and/or conduct regarding whether to rent, buy and/or finance a home.

- Knew or should have known that their "<u>express claims</u>" affected and are likely to continue to affect a consumer's decision and/or conduct regarding whether to rent, buy and/or finance a home.

- Knew or should have known that their "<u>implied claims</u>" affected and are likely to continue to affect a consumer's decision and/or conduct regarding whether to rent, buy and/or finance a home.

- Knew or should have known that their "<u>representations, omissions and practices</u>" perpetuate the belief that the mortgage interest deduction is the most significant tax benefit available annually to homeowners.

- Failed to disclose information about "<u>costs</u>" they knew or should have known affected and are likely to continue to affect a consumer's decision and/or conduct regarding whether to rent, buy and/or finance a home.

- Failed to disclose information about "<u>benefits</u>" they knew or should have known affected and are likely to continue to affect a consumer's decision and/or conduct regarding whether to rent, buy and/or finance a home.

- Failed to disclose information about "<u>restrictions</u>" they knew or should have known affected and are likely to continue to affect a consumer's decision and/or conduct regarding whether to rent, buy and/or finance a home.

- Failed to disclose information they knew or should have known affected and are likely to continue to affect a consumer's decision and/or conduct regarding whether to rent, buy and/or finance a home.

- Failed to disclose information they knew or should have known "consumers needed in order to <u>determine suitability</u>" of renting, buying and/or financing a home.

- Failed to disclose information they knew or should have known "consumers needed in order to <u>determine affordability</u>" of renting, buying and/or financing a home.

- Failed to disclose information they knew or should have known "consumers needed in order to <u>properly evaluate</u>" whether to rent, buy and/or finance a home; and

- Failed to disclose information they knew or should have known "consumers needed in order to <u>make informed choices</u>" about whether to rent, buy and/or finance a home?

NOTES:

Abusive Practices

"The hardest thing in the world to understand is the income tax"

Albert Einstein

W hile the FTC has led the way in establishing a standard for an unfair or deceptive act or practice, the *Dodd-Frank Wall Street Reform and Consumer Protection Act* (H.R.4173) recognizes what is identified as an "abusive" act or practice.

The Standard Established Under The Dodd-Frank Wall-Street Reform Act

According to the new Consumer Protection Act, an "abusive" act or practice:

(1) Materially interferes with the ability of a consumer to understand a term or condition of a consumer financial product or service; or

(2) Takes unreasonable advantage of –

    a)   A lack of understanding on the part of the consumer of the material risks, costs, or conditions of the product or service;

    b)   The inability of the consumer to protect the interests of the consumer in selecting or using a consumer financial product or service; or

    c)   The reasonable reliance by a consumer on a covered person to act in the interest of the consumer.

What do you think? Do the acts and practices of banks across America satisfy the requirements of an abusive practice under the new Consumer Protection Act?

As it relates to the first requirement listed above:

> Do the acts and practices of banks across America materially interfere with the ability of consumers to understand some very specific risks, costs and conditions associated with the mortgage interest deduction relative to the imputed rental value in relation to owner occupied housing and mortgage financing?

As it relates to requirement 2(a) listed above:

> Do acts and practices of banks across America take unreasonable advantage of consumers lack of understanding of the material risks, costs, and conditions associated with focusing on the mortgage interest deduction to the exclusion of

the imputed rental value in relation to owner occupied housing and mortgage financing?

As it relates to requirement 2(b) listed above:

Do acts and practices of banks across America take unreasonable advantage of the inability of the consumers to protect their interests when deciding between renting, owning or financing owner occupied housing?

As it relates to requirement 2(c) listed above:

Do acts and practices of banks across America take unreasonable advantage of the consumer's reasonable reliance on banks to act in the interest of consumers?

Did you answer yes to each of these questions? Surprise. Surprise.

A Basic Example of the Risks, Costs, and Conditions Associated with the Mortgage Interest Deduction

You may not have considered this basic condition associated with the mortgage interest deduction: before you can deduct the interest on your tax return, you've got to pay the interest to the bank. The bank sends you a 1098 showing all the interest you've paid during the year. If you didn't pay it, you can't deduct it.

What about a basic cost associated with the mortgage interest deduction? The money you use to pay the mortgage interest has to come from somewhere: job earnings (W-2 income or self-employed income), interest income, long-term capital gains, etc. How much do you have to earn to end up with enough to pay the mortgage interest in the first place? Below is an example that appears in *Managing Your Mortgage to Financial Independence*.

Let's take a look and see what $100 of mortgage interest actually cost.

	1 Earned W-2	2 Self Employed	3 Interest Income	4 LT Capital Gain	5 Tax Free Div.
Pay $100 In Interest	$100.00	$100.00	$100.00	$100.00	$100.00
Job Expenses	0	0	0	0	0
State & Local Taxes	0	0	0	0	0
Social Security Taxes	$9.21	$20.77	0	0	0
Medicare Taxes	$2.15	$4.86	0	0	0
Income Taxes @ 25%	$37.12	$41.88	$33.33	$17.65	$0.00
Gross Earnings	**$148.48**	**$167.50**	**$133.33**	**$117.65**	**$100**

The above example is based on a person being in the 25% marginal tax bracket. The first line shows that in each scenario (columns 1 through 5) we are paying $100 in mortgage interest. Whether or not the mortgage interest results in tax savings remains a function of your filing status and total itemized deductions compared to the standard deduction.

In all of scenarios, we are assuming that there are no state or local income taxes payable. Column one is a W-2 wage earner. Given the taxes payable on earnings, in order to net enough income to pay $100 in mortgage interest, you must have gross earning of $148.48. Column 2 is a self-employed individual. In order to net $100 to pay the mortgage interest, he or she must have gross earnings of $167.50. Column 3 shows interest income as the sole source of income. Being that there are no social security or Medicare taxes payable, this person must earn $133.33 in order to net $100. Long-term capital gains are the source of income in Column 4 and the net income must amount to $117.65 (at 15%). The source of income in Column 5 is tax-free dividend income. Since this income is tax-free it's a dollar for dollar match. However, there is another consideration with tax-free income. You can use the income to pay your mortgage interest, but you can't take the mortgage deduction.

Did You Know: Interest on bonds issued by a state or local authority that have a federal guarantee are generally not tax exempt under IRC § 149 (b)(1). An exception - interest on bonds with a guarantee from the Federal Housing Administration; Veterans Administration; Federal National Mortgage Association; Federal Home Loan Mortgage Corporation; and the Government National Mortgage Association are exempt under IRC§ 149 (b)(3)(A). Ask your investment professional when the exemption can be denied.

If There Have Been Any Abusive Practices, How Do We Assess Blame?

In the event that you want to accept the notion that third parties (non-bankers) are responsible for designing and making:

- ❑ Inaccurate calculators;
- ❑ Financially biased calculators;

- Unreliable calculators;

Or you find it reasonable to conclude that banks had nothing to do with the:

- Availability of faulty mortgage calculators;
- Placement of faulty mortgage calculators on or through their websites;
- Who accessed, accesses or uses the faulty mortgage calculators;

Then you only have to look beyond faulty mortgage calculators to some of the problems the calculators were supposed to address. For example, the typical "Rent V. Buy" (RvB) calculator indicated that it would help a consumer determine if they were "better off renting or owning" a home. The typical "Save in Tax" (SiTx) calculator indicated that it would help the consumer determine how much they could "save in taxes." Did these mortgage calculators satisfy either of those goals? If they caused more harm than good, should we expect some degree of accountability? What's the role of government in this situation? Where were the financial planners? What role have they played in this?

"Laws to gentle are seldom obeyed; too severe, seldom executed."
-Benjamin Franklin-
Statesman, author, and inventor (1706-1790)

Accountability & Transparency

"A perfection of means, and confusion of aims, seems to be our main problem."
Albert Einstein

The Standard

The Freedom of Information Act has promoted a government open to public scrutiny and oversight since it passed in 1966. In President' Obama's memorandum of January 21, 2009, regarding the Freedom of Information Act, he stated that:

> "A democracy requires accountability, and accountability requires transparency. As Justice Louis Brandeis wrote, 'sunlight is said to be the best of disinfectants.' In our democracy, the Freedom of Information Act (FOIA), which encourages accountability through transparency, is the most prominent expression of a profound national commitment to ensuring an open Government. At the heart of that commitment is the idea that accountability is in the interest of the Government and the citizenry alike.
>
> The Freedom of Information Act should be administered with a clear presumption: In the face of doubt, openness prevails. The Government should not keep information confidential

merely because public officials might be embarrassed by disclosure, because errors and failures might be revealed, or because of speculative or abstract fears. Nondisclosure should never be based on and effort to protect the personal interest of Government officials at the expense of those they are suppose to serve. In responding to request under the FOIA, executive branch agencies (agencies) should act promptly and in a spirit of cooperation, recognizing that such agencies are servants of the public.

All agencies should adopt a presumption in favor of disclosure, in order to renew their commitment to the principles embodied in the FOIA, and to usher in a new era in open Government. The presumption of disclosure should be applied to all decisions involving the FOIA.

The presumption of disclosure also means that agencies should take affirmative steps to make information public. They should not wait for specific requests from the public. All agencies should use modern technology to inform citizens about what is known and done by their Government. Disclosure should be timely."

Transparency – means that something is clear enough to see through. In government, the general motivation is to promote fairness, the public interest and the common good. The idea being that government should be transparent, participatory, and collaborative.

In President Obama's second memorandum of January 21, 2009, he directed executive departments and agencies, "to take appropriate action, consistent with law and policy, to disclose information to the public rapidly, and in a form that is easily accessible and user friendly." The Open Government Directive, issued by the Director of the Office of Management and Budget on December 8, 2009, also instructed executive departments and agencies to take specific actions to implement a transparent, collaborative, and participatory government.

Assuming that America has been led sometimes deceptively, towards the mortgage interest deduction and away from the tax benefits of the imputed rental value, what does this say about accountability and transparency on a governmental level? Was there transparency? If not, which parties should be held accountable? Because this is a tax matter, should the U.S. Treasury be held accountable in any way?

The Mortgage Interest Deduction v. Imputed Rental Value – Illustrated

Thus far I've just been telling you about the wonders of the imputed rental value. Now, let's take time to look at the numbers. For illustrative purposes, I've created three scenarios. Table 1 illustrates a home valued at $3 million. Table 2 illustrates a home valued at $175,000. And Table 3 illustrates a home valued at $350,000.

Table 1 below illustrates the federal income tax outcomes associated with column (A) buying a $3 million home with 20% down on a fixed 30 year mortgage @ 6% interest; (B) buying the home with 100% down; and column (C) renting the home at its Fair or Estimated Monthly Rental Value.

The Standard Deduction of $10,900 for married filing jointly in 2008 is illustrated for each scenario. Next, itemized expenses above the standard deduction and the corresponding tax benefit are illustrated under "taxes saved by M.I.D." Finally, the benefits associated with the Imputed

Rental Value (I.R.V) are illustrated for each scenario along with the applicable "taxes saved by I.R.V."

TABLE 1

Mortgage Interest Deduction vs. Imputed Rental Value Illustrated			
$3 Million Dollar Home	A	B	C
Property Information:	**Buyer**	**Buyer**	**Renter**
Purchase Price -	$3,000,000	$3,000,000	N/A
Down Payment -	20%	100%	N/A
Annualized Rent -	N/A	N/A	$264,000
Hazard Insurance - annually -	$10,800	$10,800	$800
Pvt. Mortgage Insurance (PMI) -	N/A	N/A	N/A
Mortgage Interest @ 6% - *	$143,198	N/A	N/A
Mortgage Term - 30 yr Fixed	30 Year	N/A	N/A
Property Taxes - Annually - **	$30,000	$30,000	N/A
Maintenance - Annually -	$25,000	$25,000	N/A
Principal Dwellers:			
John & Susie Q. Public -	**Buyer**	**Buyer**	**Renter**
Gross Annual Income -	$950,000	$950,000	$950,000
Fair Monthly Rental Value -	$22,000	$22,000	$22,000
Marginal Tax Rate -	35%	35%	35%
Gross Standard Deduction	**$10,900**	**$10,900**	**$10,900**
Taxes Saved by Std. Deduction	$3,815	$3,815	$3,815
Excess M.I.D Expenses *	**$76,865**	**$11,199**	N/A
Taxes Saved by **M.I.D**	$26,903	$3,920	N/A
Gross I.R.V Benefit:	**$55,002**	**$198,200**	**$0**
Taxes Saved by **I.R.V**	$19,251	$69,370	$0
Total Taxes Saved	**$46,153**	**$73,290**	**$0**
Average Monthly Cash Outlay	**$19,872**	**$5,483**	**$22,067**
LLM Ratio ** 5.84**	$.19	$1.11	0.00

* Please see "Notes" on next page.
** Please see "Notes" on next page.
*** Please see "Notes" on next page.
**** Please see "Notes" on next page.

Notes on $3,000,000 Dollar Example:

* Total mortgage interest amounts to $143,198 on $2.4 million dollars of mortgage debt.

** Property taxes are $30,000 for the year.

*** In column (A), because of the mortgage interest limitations, itemized (deductible) expenses consist of $59,666 of interest on the first million dollars, $6,000 attributable to the interest on $100,000 of home equity indebtedness, and $30,000 in property taxes for a total of $95,666, which is adjusted (reduced) by $7,901 because the couples income exceeds $159,950 in 2008, leaving $87,765 in mortgage interest deductible expenses. Recognizing the standard deduction of $10,900 for the couples filing status means that $76,865 is the excess or the amount attributable to the mortgage interest deduction and a corresponding or additional tax savings of $26,903 over the standard deduction. Gross Imputed Rental Value (IRV) benefit amounts to $55,002 and tax savings of $19,251. Total tax savings from the MID and the IRV over and above the standard deduction comes to **$46,153**.

In column (B) the only deductible (itemized) expense is property taxes of $30,000 and after adjusting for income and the standard deduction the excess or amount attributable to the MID is $11, 199 which corresponds to $3,920 in tax savings over an above the standard deduction. The Gross IRV benefit in column (B) amounts to a whopping $198,200 and income tax savings of over $3,920 attributable to the MID and a tremendous $69,370 as a result of the IRV for a total tax savings over and above the standard deduction of **$73,290**.

In column (C) the couple is renting the property at its Fair or Estimated Rental Value and therefore have no applicable mortgage interest deductible expenses or tax savings and no imputed rental income, tax savings or related expenses. Total tax savings over and above the standard deduction amounts to **$0**.

**** The LLM Ratio™ is intended to provide a fair, consistent, and easily communicated disclosure mechanism and reference point that not only illustrates the tax benefits associated with the mortgage interest deduction, but also those tax benefits associated with the imputed rental value. In the example above, the LLM Ratio™ of tax benefit per dollar of cash outlay is zero for the renter, $.19 for the buyer with a 20% down payment and $1.11/$1 for the all cash buyer. The LLM Ratio™ of tax benefits between scenario A & B for this couple given this property scenario is 1 to 5.84.

The MID v. IRV – Illustrated on a $175,000 Home

Table 2 below illustrates the federal income tax outcomes associated with column (A) buying a $175,000 home with 20% down on a fixed 30 year mortgage @ 5% interest; B) buying the home with 100% down; and column (C) renting the home at its Estimated or Fair Monthly Rental Value.

The Standard Deduction of $10,900 for married filing jointly in 2008 is illustrated for each scenario. Next, itemized expenses above the standard deduction and the corresponding tax benefit are illustrated under "taxes saved by M.I.D." Finally, the benefits associated with the Imputed Rental Value (I.R.V) are illustrated for each scenario along with the applicable "taxes saved by I.R.V."

TABLE 2

Mortgage Interest Deduction vs. Imputed Rental Value Illustrated			
$175,000 Dollar Home	A	B	C
Property Information:	**Buyer**	**Buyer**	**Renter**
Purchase Price -	$175,000	$175,000	N/A
Down Payment -	20%	100%	N/A
Annualized Rent -	N/A	N/A	$15,000
Hazard Insurance - annually -	$600	$600	$120
Pvt. Mortgage Insurance (PMI) -	N/A	N/A	N/A
Mortgage Interest @ 5% - *	$8,353	N/A	N/A
Mortgage Term - 30 yr Fixed	30 Year	N/A	N/A
Property Taxes - Annually - **	$1,750	$1,750	N/A
Maintenance - Annually -	$1,450	$1,450	N/A
Principal Dwellers:			
John & Susie Q. Public -	**Buyer**	**Buyer**	**Renter**
Gross Annual Income -	$65,000	$65,000	$65,000
Fair Monthly Rental Value -	$1,250	$1,250	$1,250
Marginal Tax Rate -	15%	15%	15%
Gross Standard Deduction	**$10,900**	**$10,900**	**$10,900**
Taxes Saved by Std. Deduction	$1,635	$1,635	$1,635
Excess M.I.D Expenses*	$0	$0	N/A
Taxes Saved by **M.I.D**	$0	$0	N/A
Gross I.R.V Benefit:	**$2,847**	**$11,200**	**$0**
Taxes Saved by **I.R.V**	$427	$1,680	$0
Total Taxes Saved	**$427**	**$1,680**	**$0**
Average Monthly Outlay	**$985**	**$317**	**$1,260**
LLM Ratio** 11**	$.04	$.44	0.00

* Please see "Notes" on next page.
** Please see "Notes" on next page.
*** Please see "Notes" on next page.
**** Please see "Notes" on next page

Notes on $175,000 Home Example:

*   Total mortgage interest amounts to $8,353.

**   Property taxes are $1,750 for the year.

*** In column (A), because the itemized (deductible) expenses including $8,353 in mortgage interest and $1,750 in property taxes total $10,103, which is less than the standard deduction of $10,900 for the couples filing status means that there is no tax benefit associated or attributable to the mortgage interest deduction. The Imputed Rental Value (IRV) benefit amounts to $2,847 and tax savings of **$427**, that's over and above the benefits associated with the Standard Deduction and exists even in the absence of any benefit from the MID.

Similarly, in column (B) amounts, there is no benefit associated with the MID as the itemized expenses, property taxes of $1,750, is the only item and the amount is much less than the standard deduction. On the other hand, the IRV benefit amounts to $11,200 and results in $1,680 of tax savings over and above the standard deduction and absent any benefit from the MID, resulting in total tax savings of **$1,680**.

In column (C) the couple is renting the property at its Fair or Estimated Rental Value and therefore have no applicable mortgage interest deductible expenses or tax savings and no imputed rental income, tax savings or related expenses. Total tax savings over and above the standard deduction amounts to **$0**.

**** The LLM Ratio is intended to provide a fair, consistent, and easily communicated disclosure mechanism and reference point that not only illustrates the tax benefits associated with the mortgage interest deduction, but also those tax benefits associated with the imputed rental value. In the example above, the LLM Ratio™ of tax benefits per dollar of cash outlay is zero for the renter, $.04 for the buyer with a 20% down payment and $.44 for the all cash buyer. The LLM Ratio™ of tax benefits between scenario A & B for this couple given this property scenario is 1 to 11.

The MID v. IRV – Illustrated on a $350,000 Home:

Table 3 below illustrates the federal income tax outcomes associated with column (A) buying a $350,000 home with 20% down on a fixed 30 year mortgage @ 5% interest; (B) buying the home with 100% down; and column (C) renting the home at its Fair Monthly Rental Value.

The Standard Deduction of $10,900 for married filing jointly in 2008 is illustrated for each scenario. Next, itemized expenses above the standard deduction and the corresponding tax benefit are illustrated under "taxes saved by M.I.D." Finally, the benefits associated with the Imputed Rental Value (I.R.V) are illustrated for each scenario along with the applicable "taxes saved by I.R.V."

TABLE 3

Mortgage Interest Deduction vs. Imputed Rental Value Illustrated			
$350,000 Dollar Home	A	B	C
Property Information:	**Buyer**	**Buyer**	**Renter**
Purchase Price -	$350,000	$350,000	N/A
Down Payment -	20%	100%	N/A
Annualized Rent -	N/A	N/A	$31,200
Hazard Insurance - annually -	$1,500	$1,500	$180
Pvt. Mortgage Insurance (PMI) -	N/A	N/A	N/A
Mortgage Interest @ 5% - *	$13,906	N/A	N/A
Mortgage Term - 30 yr Fixed	30 Year	N/A	N/A
Property Taxes - Annually - **	$3,500	$3,500	N/A
Maintenance - Annually -	$2,900	$2,900	N/A
Principal Dwellers:			
John & Susie Q. Public -	**Buyer**	**Buyer**	**Renter**
Gross Annual Income -	$95,000	$95,000	$95,000
Fair Monthly Rental Value -	$2,600	$2,600	$2,600
Marginal Tax Rate -	25%	25%	25%
Gross Standard Deduction	**$10,900**	**$10,900**	**$10,900**
Taxes Saved by Std. Deduction	$2,725	$2,725	$2,725
Excess M.I.D Expenses *	$6,506	$0	N/A
Taxes Saved by **M.I.D***	$1,627	$0	N/A
Gross I.R.V Benefit:	**$9,394**	**$23,300**	**$0**
Taxes Saved by **I.R.V**	$2,349	$5,825	$0
Total Taxes Saved	**$3,975**	**$5,825**	**$0**
Average Monthly Outlay	**$2,161**	**$658**	**$2,615**
LLM Ratio **** 4.93	$.15	$.74	0.00

* Please see "Notes" on next page.
** Please see "Notes" on next page.
*** Please see "Notes" on next page.
**** Please see "Notes" on next page

Notes on $350,000 Home Example:

* Total mortgage interest amounts to $13,906.

** Property taxes are $3,500 for the year.

*** In column (A), because the mortgage interest, itemized (deductible) expenses consist of $13,906 of interest and $3,500 in property taxes for a total of $17,406 of deductible expenses. Recognizing the standard deduction of $10,900 for the couples filing status means that $6,506 is the excess or the amount attributable to the mortgage interest deduction and a corresponding or additional tax savings of $1,627 over the standard deduction. Gross Imputed Rental Value (IRV) benefit amounts to $9,394 and related tax savings of $2,349. Total taxes saved from the MID and IRV amounts to **$3,975**.

In column (B) the only deductible (itemized) expense is property taxes of $3,500, which is much less than the standard deduction. On the other hand, the IRV benefit amounts to $23,300 and results in $5,825 of tax savings over and above the standard deduction and absent any benefit from the MID, resulting in total tax savings of **$5,825**.

In column (C) the couple is renting the property at its Fair or Estimated Rental Value and therefore have no applicable mortgage interest deductible expenses or tax savings and no imputed rental income, tax savings or related expenses. Total tax savings over and above the standard deduction amounts to **$0**.

**** The LLM Ratio™ is intended to provide a fair, consistent, and easily communicated disclosure mechanism and reference point that not only illustrates the tax benefits associated with the mortgage interest deduction, but also those tax benefits associated with the imputed rental value. In the example above, the LLM Ratio™ is zero tax benefit per dollar of cash outlay for the renter, $.15 per dollar of outlay for the buyers with a 20% down payment, and $.74 per dollar of outlay for the all cash buyers. The LLM Ratio ™ of tax benefits between scenario A and B for this couple given this property scenario is 1 to 4.93.

In all three of the above examples, the total taxes saved were greater for the buyer paying 100% of the purchase price for the home. And in all three examples the taxes saved due to the IRV exceeded the taxes saved due to the MID. The ratio of tax benefits to cash outlay was over seven times (5.84 +11.00+4.93=21.77/3 = **7.25**) greater for scenario B than A.

I developed the LLM Ratio™ to demonstrate the ratio of taxes saved over and above the standard deduction relative to both the MID and the IRV to the average monthly or expected relevant housing expenses applicable to financing, paying the purchase price in cash, or renting the home. By using this ratio, the consumer can now make a more informed decision about any property they choose or are considering buying or renting with fair and consistent disclosures and an apples to apples comparison. The comparison accommodates a variety of assumptions including purchase price, rental rates, down payments, interest rates, and loan terms among other items and assumption in regard to income, the property, or the economy, etc.

The U.S. Treasury

"We might hope to see the finances of the Union as clear and intelligible as a merchant's books, so that every member of Congress and every man of any mind in the Union should be able to comprehend them, to investigate abuses, and consequently to control them."
President Thomas Jefferson to Treasury Secretary Albert Gallatin, 1802

The United States Treasury serves as the home of twelve Government Bureaus, including the Mint, Engraving & Printing; Public Debt; Financial Management Services; Financial Crimes Enforcement Network; Alcohol and Tobacco Tax and Trade Bureau; Treasury Inspector General for Tax Administration; Inspector General; Community Development Financial Institutions Fund; Office of Thrift Supervision; Office of the Comptroller of the Currency; and the Internal Revenue Service.

The Treasury's stated mission is to "Maintain a strong economy and create economic and job opportunities by promoting the conditions that enable economic growth and stability at home and abroad, strengthen national security by combating threats and protecting the integrity of the financial system, and manage the U.S. Government's finances and resources effectively."

The Largest of the Treasury's Twelve Bureaus

The focus on taxes and revenues takes us to the Internal Revenue Service (IRS). The IRS is the largest of the Treasury's twelve bureaus and is responsible for determining, assessing, and collecting internal revenue in the United States.

The IRS's stated mission is to "Provide America's taxpayers top quality service by helping them understand and meet their tax responsibilities and enforce the laws with integrity and fairness to all."

The IRS believes that their mission statement describes their role and the public's expectation about how they should perform that role. Three IRS tenets are:

- In the United States, the Congress passes tax laws and requires taxpayers to comply.
- The taxpayer's role is to understand and meet his or her tax obligations.
- The IRS role is to help the large majority of compliant taxpayers with the tax law, while ensuring that the minority who are unwilling to comply pay their fair share.

Is there an Accountability Issue Here?

If one of the tenets of the IRS is to help with the tax law, should we expect this agency to provide better and more widespread information and disclosure as it relates to the estimated rental value of an owner occupied home? Should the IRS be held accountable for failing to make adequate disclosure of this tax benefit?

> "Anyone may arrange his affairs so that his taxes shall be as low as possible; he is not bound to choose that pattern which best pays the treasury. There is not even a patriotic duty to increase one's taxes. Over and over again the Courts have said that there is nothing sinister in so arranging affairs as to keep taxes as low as possible. Everyone does it, rich and poor alike and all do right, for nobody owes any public duty to pay more than the law demands."
>
> *Judge Learned Hand*

Let's go back to where this notion of imputed rental value started. In 1913, the 16th Amendment to the U.S. Constitution gave Congress the power to lay and collect taxes on income from whatever source derived without a requirement of apportionment or consideration of source. Congress then passed the United States Revenue Act of 1913.

The United States Revenue Act of 1913 gave life to the Bureau of Internal Revenue and the first 1040 became effective, which from then until now gave birth to the tax benefits we know today as the mortgage interest deduction and the imputed rental value (Estimated Rental Value minus Allowed Expenses).

The interest on personal debt had been deductible from 1913 until the Tax Reform Act of 1986, which then phased out over a period of three years the deductibility of all interest on personal indebtedness, and limited it to "qualified interest". The Estimated Rental Value of an owner only occupied home has remained unchanged since 1913.

The very first Form 1040 covered income earned between March 1, 1913 and December 31, 1913. The return plus instructions consisted of four pages. Item #2 on page three of the return, under "General Deductions", allowed the taxpayer to list "All interest paid within the year on personal indebtedness of taxpayer", thus allowing taxpayers to deduct personal interest actually paid.

Item #10 on page 4 under the heading of "Instructions" pointed out that, "Expenses for medical attendance, store accounts, family supplies, wages of domestic servants, cost of board, room, or house rent for family or personal use, *are not expenses that can be deducted from gross income*. <u>In case an individual owns his own residence he can (sic) not deduct the estimated value of his rent, neither shall he be required to include such estimated rental of his home as income.</u>" Emphasis added.

> **Only One State Has Taxed the Estimated Rental Value of Owner Occupied Property**
>
> A December 1960 article in the Journal of Finance stated that the only state to tax the estimated rental value of an owner occupied residential property in its original income tax law was Wisconsin from 1911 to 1917.

The 2006 annual report, *The State of the Nation's Housing*, released by the Joint Center for Housing Studies at Harvard University, reported that one in three American households spend more than 30 percent of income on housing, and one in seven spends more than 50 percent. Therefore, the sheer magnitude of the dollars involved makes home financing decisions one of the most significant money management decisions consumers have to make. In making those money management decisions, would knowing that the tax advantages of a paid for home compare favorably to the tax advantages of the mortgage interest deduction impact those decisions? Would investment decisions change if investors who are also mortgagors realized that a paid for home not only provides shelter, but it is also a fantastic tax shelter? Even if you needed a mortgage to acquire the home, wouldn't that knowledge help you in deciding how to manage it?

In the past 97 years, how much has the IRS done to help the majority of compliant taxpayers who have a mortgage on their primary residence understand the significance and relevance of this fundamental income tax law regarding the exclusion of the estimated rental value from income? I don't know the answer to that question, but I do know that:

- Millions of American taxpayers own homes with mortgages.

- Millions of American taxpayers with first, second, and even third mortgages on their homes are unaware of the fact that they are financially biased toward the mortgage interest deduction.

- Millions of older American taxpayers own homes with none, one or more forward mortgages that have been or are in the process of obtaining a reverse mortgage and they are unaware of the fact that they are financially biased toward the mortgage interest deduction.

- Millions of American taxpayers with one or more mortgages on their homes are unaware of the fact that there is a tax benefit currently available that is more widely available than the mortgage interest deduction.

- Millions of American taxpayers with one or more mortgages on their homes are unaware of the fact that there is a tax benefit currently available that is easier to qualify for than the mortgage interest deduction.

- Millions of American taxpayers with one or more mortgages on their homes are unaware of the fact that there is a tax benefit currently available that is more sustainable than the mortgage interest deduction.

➤ Millions of American taxpayers who are also homeowners with a mortgage are unaware of the fact that there is a tax benefit currently available that is longer lasting than the mortgage interest deduction.

➤ Millions of American taxpayers with one or more mortgages on their homes are unaware of the fact that there is a tax benefit currently available that is more valuable than the mortgage interest deduction.

➤ Millions of American taxpayers with one or more mortgages on their homes are unaware of the fact that there is a tax benefit currently available that is cheaper or significantly less costly than the mortgage interest deduction.

➤ Millions of American taxpayers with one or more mortgages on their homes are unaware of the significance of the imputed rental value or their need to understand and/or value the imputed rental value in conjunction with or independent of the mortgage interest deduction.

➤ Millions of American taxpayers with one or more mortgages on their homes are unaware of how focusing on the mortgage interest deduction alone can negatively impact their income, increase their financial risks, increase their income taxes, increase their overall housing costs, prolong retirement, and be at odds with their actual intentions or financial plans.

> Millions of American taxpayers with a mortgage on their homes unwittingly, among other things, pay more than their fair share of taxes.

> Millions of American taxpayers are victims of unfair, deceptive and abusive housing, tax and financial practices as a result of this issue not getting the "sunlight" alluded to by Justice Brandeis.

Given this set of circumstances, how much do you think the IRS has done to help the majority of compliant taxpayers who have a mortgage on their primary residence understand the significance and relevance of the fundamental income tax law regarding the exclusion of the estimated rental value from income?

What Taxpayers Services Does the IRS Provide?

The taxpayer services provided by the IRS involve pre-filing, education, filing a return and account services.

For fiscal year 2009, 20% of the IRS's budget or over $2,300,000,000 ($2.3 Billion) focused on what the IRS calls taxpayer services (pre-filing, education, filing and account services).

For fiscal year 2009, the IRS processed 144 million individual tax returns, of which ~95 million where filed electronically.

For fiscal year 2009, the IRS did not process a single individual tax return for a domestic American civilian based on the IRV of an owner only occupied principal residence.

The IRS also provides enforcement of the tax laws, including investigations, examinations and collections.

Enforcement receives the lion share of the IRS budget for fiscal year 2009 at 44% or over $5,148,000,000 ($5.148 billion).

For fiscal year 2009, the IRS had 6,821,000 delinquent accounts and that it started 2,211,000 new investigations.

For fiscal year 2009, the IRS had no delinquent individual tax return or new investigation of a single individual tax return for a domestic American civilian based on the IRV of an owner only occupied principal residence.

Additionally, the IRS provides operational support including infrastructure, shared services and support, and information systems, including infrastructure, shared services & support, information system.

For fiscal year 2009, the IRS expended 33% of its budget or over $3,861,000,000 ($3.8 billion) on operational support.

More Than 80% of Revenues Collected by the IRS Comes From Individual Taxpayers

- ❖ More than 80% of the IRS's revenue comes from individual taxpayers.[4]
- ❖ More than 80% of the IRS's budget covers personnel & benefits costs[5].
- ❖ In fiscal 2009, the IRS's average compensation and benefits cost per employee rounded out to $80K a year ($79,115).

What is the Taxpayer's Role?

The taxpayer's role is quite simply to understand and meet his or her tax obligations.

Is there any evidence that the IRS Really Perceives the Imputed Rental Value (IRV) To Be A Tax Benefit?

You may still think the IRV as a tax benefit maybe a lot to do about nothing, and that the IRV tax benefit is an obscure or theoretical benefit that the Internal Revenue Service doesn't concern itself with. In order to demonstrate that the IRV as a tax benefit is not an academic or theoretical exercise or an esoteric tax benefit that the IRS has not been concerned about since 1913, I'll use a situation that occurred at Harvard University and some other universities as an example.

Harvard University has the distinction of being:

- ➤ The oldest institution of higher learning in America (1636).
- ➤ The first corporation chartered in America (1650).
- ➤ The best endowed university in America ($25.6 billion).
- ➤ One of the most respected & prestigious universities in America today.

The IRS as part of its review of executive compensation practices and possible reporting inconsistencies at various colleges & universities required the institutions to list the rental value of university provided housing on the applicable tax forms. Harvard University's tax return shows that the $8,044 monthly rental value of the university provided housing increased, Drew G. Faust's 2008 annual income by $96,537, bringing her total compensation to over $822,000.

Some real estate agents would argue that the mansion at 33 Elmwood Ave in Cambridge Massachusetts should go for about $12,000 a month[6]. The principle applies for other college and university presidents around the country whose principal residence is provided by a college or university, as Boston's University President Robert A. Brown knows all to well. The rental value of his university provided residence on 135 Ivy Street was valued at over $257,447 annually, putting his total compensation over $1,043,392. In June 2010, the Boston Globe reported that the IRS is in the midst of conducting an audit of more than 30 colleges and universities focusing on executive compensation and analyzing possible reporting inconsistencies. In any case, from this you should see the beauty of the example as it involves (1) the IRV of a property, (2) a non-owner occupied property, and how the IRS applies the law to an alternate fact pattern (after all it is the taxpayer's role to understand the law). As you can see from this example, the IRS is keenly aware of the tax benefits of a property. The question is: Is it the role of the IRS to make sure taxpayers are as keenly aware of this benefit as they are?

Conflicts of Interest

"History shows that where ethics and economics come in conflict, victory is always with economics. Vested interests have never been known to have willingly divested themselves unless there was sufficient force to compel them."
B.R. Ambedkar (Indian Politician and founder of the Indian Constitution)

T his Unit focuses on (identifying) several specific financial and strategic conflicts of interest that exist between consumers (who want to make intelligent, informed housing tax and financial decisions) who expect to be treated honestly and fairly by their banks, and the strategic business interests of those financial institutions. Banks and other financial services providers have a proven propensity to perpetuate the belief that the mortgage interest deduction is the most advantageous or significant tax benefit available annually to millions of American homeowners, which of course plays into their business goal of selling mortgages, insurance and other investments.

While all conflicts of interest aren't always evidence of an unfair or deceptive act or practice, it's safe to conclude that anytime you have an unfair or deceptive act or practice, there is an excellent chance you'll find evidence of a conflict of interest (COI). This Unit isn't focused on passing judgment as it relates to labeling a particular act or practice as immoral or unethical only in pointing out that it offends established public policy, existing laws or regulations and/or the interest of individual consumers, and exploits financially biased consumers in particular. The goal here is to enable consumers to recognize that specific acts or practice are or can cause consumers substantial financially injury.

Recognizing That A Conflict of Interests Exists

The reality is that in order to be able to protect your self-interest, you need to be aware of what your interests are. Millions of consumers aren't aware of the fact that when it comes to making intelligent, informed, housing, tax and financial decisions, they have or could have a conflict of interest with their bank, mortgage company, and other financial services providers.

Conflict of Interest: A situation where an individual could act counter to an obligation, duty or expectation to act in the best interest of another, as there's an opportunity to exploit the relationship or position of trust for personal benefit.

It is understandable that as consumers, we sometimes lack sufficient knowledge to decipher the immediate impacts of our financial decisions, not to mention how those decisions will impact our ability to satisfy other financial responsibilities and goals. During these times, we turn to the financial professionals who are supposed to be experts in the area, but how do we differentiate between those who are providing information as part of a marketing strategy from those who are providing solid objective information, even when the outcome of educating us runs contrary to their business goal of making a sale?

When you are in the market for a home, you are likely to come in contact with one or more of the following people:

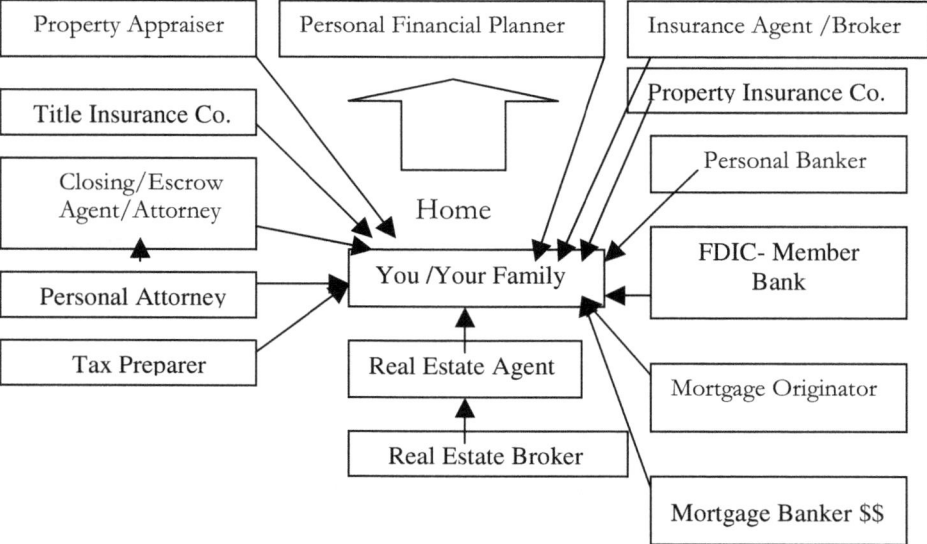

Which one of these professionals discussed with you any aspect of the mortgage interest deduction? No doubt, it was most of them. Which one of these professionals discussed with you any aspect of the imputed rental value? Which one of these professionals is required by rules, regulations or the law to disclose to you the tax benefits of the IRV?

<u>Three Reasons Why</u>

<u>These Parties Aren't Touting The Tax Benefits of The IRV</u>

<u>During The Home Selection Process</u>

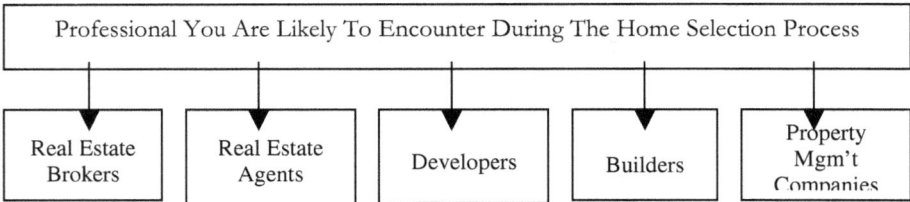

Professional You Are Likely To Encounter During The Home Selection Process

Real Estate Brokers	Real Estate Agents	Developers	Builders	Property Mgm't Companies

Q. When it comes to home purchasing, what is the primary goal of the parties listed above?

A. To sell you whatever home you are ready, willing or able to buy, right? Moreover, the incentive to do that is due to how they are compensated.

The $ Incentive[1]

1. The Incentive – How are these parties primarily compensated?

Percentage (%) of Total Sales Price[2]

2. Percentage (%) of Total Sales Price – Generally, the amount of compensation or profit received by one of the above parties is

based on the total sales price of the property or the annualized rental amount.

The Higher The Percentage 1%, 2%, or 3%-7%	The Larger The Sales Price/Amount

3. The greater the commission percentage (%) or the larger the total sales price, the greater the compensation incentive because as the percentage of the sales price increases and/or the larger the total sales price or rental amount, the greater the total compensation.

The more homes sold and the higher the sales price, all else being equal, the greater the total compensation. Thus, real estate agents/brokers, developers and builders have an incentive to sell more homes at higher prices.

Here are three examples based on the diagram and information below:

A	B	C	D
$100,000 Home 5% Comp. = $5,000	$150,000 Home 5% Comp. = $7,500	$200,000 Home 5% Comp. = $10,000	$500,000 Home 5% Comp. = $25,000

#1 – Assuming the home sales prices as stated for homes A, B, C, and D, the commission on the sale would be as follows: A = $5,000; B = $7,500; C= $10,000; & D = $25,000.

#2 – Assuming one person sold all of the homes, he or she would
receive the total commissions for all of the homes: $5,000+
$7,500 + $10,000 + $25,000 for a grand total of $47,500.

Let's assume that the buyers in this first example have $300,000 cash
that they are willing to use to purchase a house. This couple is ten
years away from retirement and is looking for a home just for
themselves. They have excellent credit and are above average wage
earners who think the mortgage interest deduction provides tax savings
that will lower their tax burden. They like Homes B and C, which they
could pay for cash. However, they also like Home D, but that would
require obtaining a mortgage to pay the difference. The sales
agent/broker and builder/developer haven't made a sale in six months
and are very short on prospects. What do you think they would advise
this couple to do? Do you think that advice would differ if the
agent/broker and builder/developer were aware of the tax benefits
associated with the imputed rental value on an owner occupied home?
Do you think anyone would disclose that there are tax benefits
associated with a paid for home?

In this next example, assume that two retired couples are looking to
buy houses in the same neighborhood. One of the couples has enough
money to pay cash to purchase Home A and the other has enough
money to pay cash to purchase Home B. These couples have been
friends for thirty years and are willing to pool their cash towards a
down payment on Home D even though it's more space than they
actually need and it would require obtaining a mortgage. Which

home(s) do you think these couples would be advised to purchase? Do you think that advice would differ if the agent/broker and builder/developer were aware of the tax benefits associated with the imputed rental value on an owner occupied home? Do you think anyone would disclose that there are tax benefits associated with a paid for home?

For this last example, assume that the potential buyer is a young newly married couple. They currently live in an apartment that they love and the rent is only $500 per month. The couple has just started a new business so their combined annual income is only $25,000. They are considering buying Home A because they've heard that the mortgage interest deduction will save money on their taxes, which will make buying this home affordable for them. They are concerned that with little money down, the mortgage on Home A will have a monthly payment of $1,000 per month, which doubles their current housing costs so they are really counting on the tax savings from the mortgage interest deduction to make the payment affordable. Do you think the agent/broker and builder/developer will play up the benefits of the mortgage interest deduction in making this home affordable or will they advise this couple to continue to rent for now?

Given the incentive to sell more versus fewer properties, the agent/broker/builder could advise, encourage or simply suggest that a prospective homeowner obtain a mortgage for the difference in the dollar amount needed to purchase the property under consideration.

1. They are paid a commission.

2. The more they sell, the more they are paid (new or resale for whatever reason).

3. There are <u>no charge backs of commissions</u> once a sale is made. <u>The same property can be sold again & again,</u> a resale is a resale. It doesn't matter the reason/season.

I've already given away the answer to this question, but which tax benefit (MID) or (IRV) is more inline with the goal and incentive of the first group of professionals you are likely to encounter during the home purchase transaction? When it comes to non-mandatory disclosure of information that might negatively impact the sale and the size of the commission, do you think the financial incentives of these professionals will be more inline with the buyers of the property or with those entities providing the financing of the property?

Three Reasons Why

Mortgage Providers Aren't Touting The Tax Benefits of The IRV

Restoring American Financial Stability is all about a new independent watchdog housed at the Federal Reserve with the authority to ensure that American consumers get clear, accurate information when they shop for such things as a mortgage and other financial products. The idea is to protect American consumers from hidden fees, abusive terms and deceptive practices.

It is my contention that the lack of clarity or accurate information, hidden fees, abusive terms and deceptive practices can be summed up in one word, marketing. In America, we hand out awards annually for the best commercial. We love marketing.

Marketing is about moving goods and services from producer to end user or consumer.

From a consumer's perspective, who provides or supplies the consumer marketplace with mortgages?

> Mortgage Originators*

*Mortgage Providers/Supplier are Known as Originators and Include:

State & Federally Chartered Banks	State & Federally Chartered Credit Unions	State Licensed Mortgage Bankers	Mortgage Brokers/ Loan Officers

1. Compensation

One reason mortgage providers or originators don't promote the tax benefits of the imputed rental value could be due to their primary method of compensation.

If you never have a mortgage (for any reason in the world), then no state or federally chartered bank or credit union, loan officer or mortgage broker, or mortgage servicers or related entities earned any mortgage origination related compensation. (Look at who's paid on a mortgage.) There are no discount points, origination fees, service release fees, yield spread premiums, credit report fees, appraisal fees, pest inspection fees, transfer taxes, recording fees, processing fees, documentation fees, loan closing costs of any kind paid to any entity if there is no mortgage loan.

There's some truth to the old adage that nothing happens until somebody sells something.

2. Timing

There are more reasons why mortgage providers and originators don't promote the tax benefits of the imputed rental value. Anytime you talk about a mortgage, you have to recognize what I like to call the great equalizer - time. First, the mortgage interest deduction provides the homebuyer an incentive to buy a home sooner than he or she would if they waited to accumulate sufficient funds to purchase a house for cash. Second, if people waited to accumulate sufficient cash to purchase a home, the primary mortgage market (where buyers negotiate the terms of a mortgage) would be eliminated and thus mortgage originators & bankers wouldn't be compensated in this regard, as the need would be eliminated. A third reason related to time and why mortgage originators don't promote the tax benefits of the imputed rental value is that bankers like to receive fee and interest income. The longer you take to pay a mortgage off the greater the interest and fee income received. Fourth, mortgage originators are not paid by the hour or for the amount of time they spend educating you. They are generally paid for the number and size or volume of mortgage sales made. Fifth, mortgage originators and providers know that the tax benefits associated with a fixed rate amortized mortgage will dwindle to zero over-time, whereas all else being equal, the benefits associated with the imputed rental value will grow and compensate the mortgagor (borrower) for any reductions in tax benefits associated with mortgage interest expenses. Thus, the seventh reason related to time and why mortgage originators and producers don't mention the tax benefits related to the imputed rental value is that the imputed rental value is simply longer lasting, initially less costly and cheaper to sustain than the mortgage interest deduction over any relevant period of time, resulting in fewer mortgages.

3.   Frequency

Experience suggests that frequency from the practical perspective of a mortgage originator and provider is the opportunity to be paid again and again for originating up to five or six mortgage loans of one kind or another over a typical adults lifetime.

Originators know from experience and observation that consumers move every five to seven years and that the economy fluctuates, interest rates move up and down, businesses go through the boom and bust cycles and the federal government attempts to guide the economy via various fiscal and monetary policies and strategies.

Even more specifically, originators and providers know taxes are a consideration when it comes to either purchasing or financing a home as there are property taxes, transfer taxes, or income taxes of one kind or another associated with every real property transaction. Millions of properties are sold, bought and mortgaged every month and taxes, documentation, disclosures and IRS Forms are a part of almost every single one of the transactions. While the seller generally receives IRS Form 1099-S, the mortgagor a.k.a the borrower will complete, receive and/or sign at least three or four IRS Forms.

With regular frequency, the mortgagor/borrower will receive IRS Form W-9 authorizing the lender to verify the borrower's social security number. The closing attorney will usually make a joke something to the effect that "you want to make sure this is right so that you get proper credit in relation to all that mortgage interest." The borrower/mortgagor may also be asked to complete and/or sign IRS Form 4506 authorizing the lender to receive a copy of the borrower's tax returns and once a year the borrower will receive IRS Form 1098 that indicates, among other things, the amount of mortgage interest paid for the year.

Unfortunately, receipt of some of the above tax forms at closing and others throughout the life of the mortgage loan with no factual reference or disclosure of the imputed rental value essentially reinforces and perpetuates your financial bias towards the mortgage interest deduction.

Parties the Buyer Encounters Have No Incentive to Promote the Imputed Rental Value

As I've illustrated, all parties (other than the buyer) to a home purchase transaction have an incentive to favor the positive aspects of the mortgage interest deduction to the exclusion of the imputed rental value.

Developers and Builders - have an interest in promoting a benefit that encourages you to get financing because it enables you to buy something that you may not otherwise purchase now. A calculator that over states the tax benefit, encourages, reinforces, or provides another reason to purchase a home, and to purchase one sooner than later. Such a calculator can positively impact the number of homes sold. The consumer is disadvantaged, not the builder.

Real Estate Agents and Brokers - Same scenario, they generally are paid only when a home is bought or sold. A calculator that over states the tax benefit, encourages, reinforces, or provides another reason to purchase a home and possibly an even bigger one. Such a calculator can positively impact the number and size of sales. Not telling a user the difference between the calculators or about the IRV generally when discussing the MID promotes a financial bias, an unfair, deceptive and abusive financial practice as well as a possible conflict of interest as consumers don't generally expect their real estate agents and brokers (who may be acting as fiduciaries) to be financially biased. Here again, the consumer is disadvantaged, not the real estate agent or broker.

Mortgage Bankers and Originators - Same scenario, they generally are paid only when a home is financed or refinanced. A calculator that over states the tax benefit, encourages, reinforces, or provides another reason to finance or refinance a home. Such a calculator can positively impact the number and size of home mortgages. Not telling a user the difference between the calculators or about the IRV generally when discussing the MID promotes a financial bias, an unfair, deceptive and an abusive financial practice as well as a possible conflict of interest, as consumers don't generally expect calculators or financial professionals (who may be acting as fiduciaries) to be financially biased. The consumer is disadvantaged, not the mortgage banker or originator.

Others:

Broker/Dealers & Investment Professionals - Same scenario, they are generally are paid a fee or commission when an investment is purchased, sold or managed. A calculator that over states the tax benefit of financing or refinance a home increases home financing, which increases the amount of funds available for investment purposes because those funds are not going towards the purchase price. Not telling a customer or client about the IRV when discussing the MID promotes a financial bias, an unfair, deceptive and an abusive financial practice as well as a possible conflict of interest, as consumers don't generally expect calculators or financial professionals (who may be acting as fiduciaries) to be engaged in unfair, deceptive or abusive financial practices.

Property & Casualty Insurance - Agents & Broker Same scenario. They generally are paid only when an insurance policy is sold or renewed. A calculator that over states the tax benefit of financing or refinance a home increases the number of financings, and (1) increases the amount of insurance coverage required as the mortgagee requires coverage sufficient to protect their security interests, (2) improves client retention as premiums are paid from escrow and (3) less shopping for better coverage/lower premiums at renewal. There's also deterrence against lower annual premiums because people are less inclined to be self-insured or opt for higher deductibles. Not telling a customer or client about the IRV when discussing the MID promotes a financial bias, an unfair, deceptive and an abusive financial practice as well as a possible conflict of interest, as consumers don't generally expect calculators or their insurance agent/consultant (who may be acting as a fiduciary) to be engaged in unfair, deceptive or abusive financial services practices. The consumer's insurance agent isn't or hasn't typically been a source of mortgage funding, but this is changing. The consumer is disadvantaged, not the P&C agent or broker.

If the parties mentioned thus far do not have an incentive to make you aware of the tax benefits of the IRV, who does?

NOTES:

We're Financial Planners and We're Here To Help You Really?

"We cannot solve our problems with the same thinking we used when we created them."
Albert Einstein

The original idea behind comprehensive or broad based financial planning was avoiding the gaps or financial inefficiencies that often resulted from fragmented, piecemeal or segmented planning brought on by starts, stops, miscommunications and changes in circumstances. Towards this end, the distinguishing feature between financial planning and everything else was that financial planning was first and foremost a process that focused on helping a client articulate and ultimately achieve their personal financial goals independent of any company or particular financial product.

As stated in the <u>ABC's of Mortgaged Based Financial Planning</u>:

> "A comprehensive financial planner considers a client's goals and objectives, personal circumstances, tax situation, risk-exposures, risk tolerance and outlook when creating a financial plan. The focus and the process are always supposed to be client centered. The planner's role was and has been basically to make recommendations for growing and preserving wealth, minimizing taxes, planning an estate, planning for retirement, college funding, major purchases, among other things, depending on the needs of the particular client."

Did You know: There are no laws regulating financial planning as a profession in the United States of America. Because there are no laws regulating financial planning as a profession, there are no minimum or mandatory educational, experience, examination or ethical requirements to enter into the general practice of personal financial planning.

Different Names Promote Games

It is very difficult to differentiate between financial planning professionals, professional financial planning pretenders, the incompetent and/or the unethical financial planning practitioner based upon any title or credential. Unlike an accountant, attorney or medical doctor, a financial planner may choose to go by a variety of titles including financial advisor, consultant, counselor, wealth planner, etc. and may hold one, none or a variety of financial designations.

The only sure bet is that regardless of what financial practitioners choose to called themselves, or the designations they hold that may or may not reflect what they do, the one thing you can bank on is that neither the incompetent nor the unethical will label themselves as such.

In order to reduce the possibility of consumer confusion and overcome the inability to differentiate between practitioners, while endeavoring to avoid unfair, deceptive and predatory financial planning practices, it is recommended that you give no adviser a free pass. You should examine all practitioners the same way.

Start by asking yourself the same basic question: Can you reasonably expect someone whose primary focus is to sell you a financial product to voluntarily disclose to you a tax benefit, when if pursued, will drastically diminish the amount of discretionary funds you have available to buy their product(s)?

Failing to Differentiate Product Sales From Advisory Services

It is estimated that less than 3% of all financial planning practitioners practice personal financial planning as a separate and distinct function from other financial services (fee for service basis). Thus 97% of all financial planning practitioners are involved in providing some other services. There is virtually no limit as to what those other services can be. Some of the most common or popular but not required financial services combinations include asset management, annuity sales, investment advice, insurance sales, security sales, college, employee benefit, estate, retirement, and tax planning. Advisory services can be broken down by (1) general (comprehensive – broad based) personal financial advice, (2) personal financial advice about one or more focused concerns or related product areas identified above, which could be independent of selling the product(s), and (3) personal financial advice provided in contemplation of selling a financial product.

Often financial planning gets intermingled with other financial services because, as a practical matter, holders of financial planning credentials may not practice financial planning 100% of the time or they may not practice at all, and they may not provide financial planning services on a 100% fee-only basis. To reduce the possibility of consumer and practitioner confusion, advice or advisory services should be separate and distinct or simply independent of any other service the planner may provide, thus supporting the development of personal financial planning as a separate and distinct profession and reducing the probability of fraud by those who use the financial advisory or planning moniker to take advantage of the consumers' need for advisory services primarily to sell or manage other financial products.

In April 2009, the managing director of public policy for the CFP Board, Marilyn Mohrman-Gillis stated that, "There is a huge regulatory gap," and that "Consumers and investors are being defrauded by 300,000 people who are saying that they are financial planners or financial advisors, when in fact, they are basically selling product" [7]

Intellectually Dishonesty is defined as avoiding an honest, deliberate and comprehensive approach to a matter because it may introduce an adverse effect on personally and professionally held views and beliefs. Over the last five years alone more than ninety percent (90%) of the CFP Board's programs and service revenues came from CFP® Certificants/practitioners and those who want to be.

The Financial Planning Process

The CFP Board defines the financial planning process as typically including, but not limited to, some or all of the following six elements or steps:

- ➢ 1st Step/element – Establishing and defining the planner client relationship,
- ➢ 2nd Step/element - Gathering client data & goals,
- ➢ 3rd Step/element - Analyzing & evaluating the client's financial data & goals,
- ➢ 4th Step/element - Developing & presenting recommendations and/or alternatives,
- ➢ 5th Step/element - Implement the planning recommendations, and
- ➢ 6th Step/element - Monitoring the planning recommendations.

The Financial Planning Promise

At some point between meeting with a financial planner and contracting or agreeing to work with a typical financial planner, the planner may have explained the financial planning process, how they operate, and what they do. At some point and in one-way or another, they explicitly express or imply that they will follow the financial planning process with the client's data, objectives and goals in mind. The financial planning promise is that they individually, and/or in concert with others, will work in the client's interests, with the client's concerns and goals in mind. The personal financial planning process doesn't immediately invoke the buyer beware mentality, but it does invoke the financial planning promise; and the financial planning promise supports and implies, at a minimum, suitability and depending on the facts and circumstances, even a fiduciary standard of care.

The Standard That Applies & Matters

The standard that applies and matters most, after covering the basic financial planning process from the consumer's, customer's, or client's perspective, is not a suitability or fiduciary standard, but whether or not what the practitioner said they would or won't do is in line with what they actually do or don't do. The bottom line being, does what they say match what they do and does it honor the personal financial planning promise?

Within the financial services industry there are two broad standards that are applied to the services of most financial services professionals, a suitability standard and a fiduciary standard. Registered Representatives (includes, inter-alia, stockbrokers, and investment company representatives such as mutual fund salespeople, variable annuities or variable life insurance agents) are generally judged on the basis of suitability. For example, was this financial product, suggestion or recommendation suitable for this client? Registered Investment Advisers (RIAs) are generally judged on the basis of a fiduciary standard, which generally requires, among other things, that conflicts of interest be disclosed to the client, and asks the question of whether the financial product, suggestion, recommendation or action was in the client's best interest.

When it comes to financial planners, there is no national standard because the practice of personal financial planning is generally not regulated outside the accounting, insurance, investment, legal and securities world. Depending on the specialty (insurance, investments, etc.) of the financial planner they could be held to a suitability or fiduciary standard by that industry. Some financial planners voluntarily adopt the higher fiduciary standard. What's actually much more important and relevant than the standard a financial planning practitioners claims is how they treat and provide benefit to their clients. The financial planning promise is all about following the financial planning process to address your needs, objectives, goals and concerns. It's supposed to be using the process in order to look out for you, but whether financial planners do or not has never been tested.

As noted in the book, *ABC's of Mortgaged Based Financial Planning*:

"It has become trendy to use the words 'planner' or 'planning' as bait to entice consumers to buy financial products including mortgages. Some tactics marketed to practitioners include 'well-named' marketing credentials that are meant to convey a sense of knowledge and professionalism to the consumer. Catchy phrases and terminology are developed that tend to give a false impression of the benefits to consumers.

Research shows that confusion still exists among the consuming public regarding the differences between financial planning as a process and other financial services. Consumer confusion my result from FSPs who identify themselves to the consuming public as financial planners although their main purpose is to sell financial products while giving little, if any, regard to applying the six step financial planning process.

These kinds of marketing ploys add to consumer confusion further diminishing the degree of trust consumers attach to the words 'planner' and 'planning'."

Did You Know: That the two largest groups in terms of raw numbers of designated financial planning practitioners in the United States are Certified Financial Planners (CFPs) approximate 58,000 and Chartered Financial Consultants (ChFCs) 48,000.

Where Did the Financial Planner Receive Their Financial Planning Education?

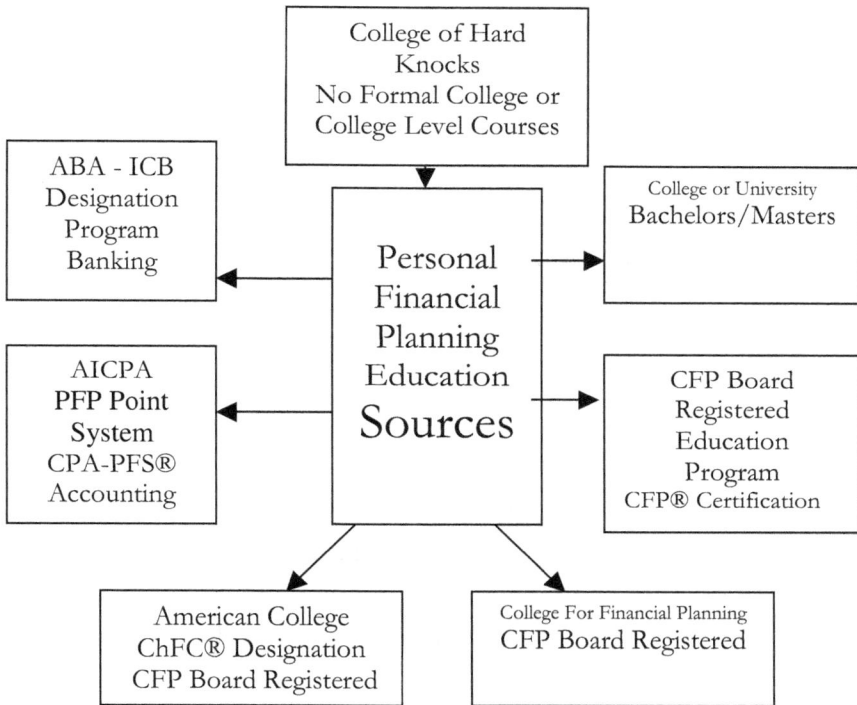

```
                    ┌─────────────────────┐
                    │   College of Hard   │
                    │       Knocks        │
                    │ No Formal College or│
                    │ College Level Courses│
                    └─────────────────────┘
┌──────────────┐              │
│  ABA - ICB   │              ▼
│ Designation  │    ┌──────────────────┐    ┌──────────────────┐
│   Program    │    │                  │    │ College or University│
│   Banking    │◄───│     Personal     │───►│ Bachelors/Masters │
└──────────────┘    │    Financial     │    └──────────────────┘
                    │    Planning      │
┌──────────────┐    │    Education     │    ┌──────────────────┐
│   AICPA      │    │                  │    │    CFP Board     │
│  PFP Point   │◄───│     Sources      │───►│   Registered     │
│   System     │    │                  │    │   Education      │
│  CPA-PFS®    │    └──────────────────┘    │    Program       │
│  Accounting  │        │         │         │ CFP® Certification│
└──────────────┘        ▼         ▼         └──────────────────┘
          ┌──────────────────┐ ┌──────────────────────────┐
          │ American College │ │College For Financial Planning│
          │ ChFC® Designation│ │   CFP Board Registered   │
          │CFP Board Registered│ └──────────────────────────┘
          └──────────────────┘
```

Differentiation Based Upon The Purpose of Certfication

Just a Thought: *As a consumer, you've got to keep the proper perspective. Certification in Personal Financial Planning much like accreditation for colleges and universities is a voluntary, self-regulatory, peer review, non-governmental process.*

Certification is a form of credentialing, and it is common for those who have met the requirements of the organization granting the credential to have the right to indicate that fact for a specific period of time, with a certification mark, which may include post-nominal letters. The Institute of Certified Bankers points out on it's website that, "Industry based certification is often accepted and encouraged by government agencies because it provides a set of high standards consistently maintained which ultimately benefit the public when developed and managed appropriately."

The most commonly stated purpose of certification is to:

1. Establish a recognized minimal level of knowledge and competency in personal financial planning.
2. Give a professional recognition to those who have met certain educational, experience, examination and/or ethical standards.
3. Provide the public (potential customers, clients and employers) with a means of identifying competent, ethical and experienced Personal Financial Planners.
4. Promote professional and ethical practices by enforcing adherence to a code of conduct or ethics.
5. Promote ongoing professional continued education and professional development.

An Alternative Purpose of Certification in Personal Financial Planning

When an individual pursues and earns a certification, they are indirectly documenting that they have met certain educational, experience, examination and/or ethical standards. A consumer, potential customer, client, an employer or other person can generally verify whether or not a person holds a particular credential or designation as indicated. Like a college degree, a certification, designation, or credential acts a medium of exchange. It signifies an achievement/accomplishment or adherence to "something" and communicates that to those who recognize the certification marks.

A number of articles in trade journals and even the popular press have expressed the position that there are many in the field of personal financial planning that may have pursued a particular designation for marketing purposes because of what it is supposed to represent. While I believe that the marketing of a designation is reasonable and expected, a credential can communicate the four P's of marketing. A credential can promote or signify the availability of a particular product or service, at a particular place and time, and at various price points. What I see as a problem is when the certification mark is used as a proxy, inter-alia, for quality, integrity, and mutual respect. In this instance, the public is taught to recognize a particular mark and will give it respect based upon what it is supposed to represent as opposed to the respect that the individual deserves. When an individual graduates it states on the diploma, degree, or credential that the awarding entity recognizes the individual for having satisfied the requirements for the particular diploma, degree or designation and as a result is entitled to all associated rights, honors and privileges. The credential establishes instant credibility, you don't have to explain it as the qualification is understood and immediately communicated by those who know. Similar to what a college Bachelor's, Masters' or PhD degree or MD communicates.

> **Did You Know**: That in 2007 the American College announced via a press release that it had its 10,000[th] CFP® student. Since then, the American College claims to be the "#1 Provider of CFP® Certification Education" in the USA and a leading provider of textbooks to CFP® approved education programs.

Certification/Claims of Achievement No Substitute for Actual Achievement in PFP

While a certification program can have intentions and aspirations, it is suppose to represent that an individual has met certain educational, experience, examination and/or ethical standards. The organizations that grant or otherwise award the certification should be held to the same standards it requires of its designees or certificants. Excellence isn't automatically attained by its mere mention.

Any organizations that claim excellence or a particular achievement should be able to disclose, document, and demonstrate evidence of those claims so that objective parties can inspect and/or evaluate all such claims. No matter how many claims are made, claims of achievement are no substitute for integrity, respect and actual achievements, which improves quality of service and results.

Quick - View
Summary of Three Nationally Recognized Programs
Awarding Comprehensive Financial Planning Designations

CFP Board Awards CFP®	American College Awards ChFC®	American Institute of CPAs Awards CPA-PFS®
Organization	Organization	Organization
Obliged to Serve: Public Interest IRS Code Section: 501(c)(3)	Obliged to Serve: Public Interest IRS Code Section: 501(c)(3)	Obliged to Serve: Member's Interest IRS Code Section: 501(c)(6)
Tax Deductible Contributions No Membership Dues Certification Fees	Tax Deductible Contributions No Membership Dues Certification Fees	No Tax Deductible Contributions Membership Dues* Certification Fees

*Membership dues and/or certification fees maybe deducted as a business expense.

Did You Know: Only two CFP Board registered colleges and universities in the U.S. award the Doctor of Philosophy (Ph.D.) (the highest recognized research degree) in Personal Financial Planning. The eldest of the two Ph.D. programs in the country is at Texas Tech University (it started as a minor in Personal Financial Planning). The program is funded in part by the largest grant ever awarded by the CFP Board, one million nine hundred thousand dollars ($1,900,000). By way of contrast, the American College does not offer either the Ph.D. or any other doctorate.

CFPs Are Held Out As Being The Single Largest Self-Regulatory Group of Personal Financial Planners in America

In fact, the CFP Board represents:

1.   That its policies and positions are compensation neutral.

2. That CFP Certificant's recommendations are compensation neutral.

3. That CFP Certificants are and have been willing to disclose and fairly manage conflicts of interest.

4. That CFP Certificants are and have been competent to provide financial planning services.

5. That CFP Certificants engage in full and fair disclosure of material facts.

6. That CFP Certificants would never knowingly or intentionally mislead client's they advise (*or fail to fairly disclose material facts necessary for informed decision making*).

7. That CFP Certificants provide professional financial planning services with *integrity, objectively, and competency,* while being *fair* and *reasonable* in all their professional relationships by d*isclosing conflicts of interest, protecting the confidentiality of all client information,* acting in a manner that *demonstrates exemplary professional conduct* while providing professional services *diligently.*

8. That Certificants have special qualifications in the area of Personal Financial Planning (PFP).

9.   That Certificants have adequate PFP experience.

10.   That Certificants have adequate PFP education.

11.   That Certificants are committed to behaving professionally.

12.   That Certificants are committed to acting ethically.

13.   That Certificants have been adequately examined.

14.   That Certificants have special knowledge of (or insight into) the issues faced by existing or potential customers, clients, or investors.

15.   That Certificants not only agree to maintain compliance with the CFP® Board's Code of Conduct but actually do comply as they have over 60,000 Certificants that have not been admonished, reprimanded, suspended or had their use of the CFP® designation revoked.

16.   That Certificants have the ability to provide financial planning services unsupervised and in compliance with the Boards code of conduct.

17.   That the CFP Board has properly and adequately supervised the activities of CFP Certificants in compliance with its own

policies, procedures, rules of conduct and professional responsibilities.

18.   That from 1985 to the present, the CFP Board of Standards, Inc. has benefited the public by granting certificants the right to use the CFP® certification mark.

A fairly big deal is made about the source, the amount of study received, the ethical standards, and the level of experience required to be a holder of these designations, but none of this comes with a money back guarantee or any other type guarantee.

Do you know which of these designations indicates that the holder must disclose to clients and prospective clients the existence and the tax benefits of the IRV as part of their financial planning service? That's right, none of them.

Historically, financial planners have left consumers to their own devices in making mortgage-financing decisions. In recent times, there are many financial experts who have gotten rich spreading the word that the best way to accumulate wealth is by using the wealth buildup in the home and by obtaining and maintaining the largest mortgage possible in order to invest money elsewhere. Other financial planners just work around the mortgage when identifying discretionary funds available for investments and other financial products

As stated in <u>The Book on Mortgage Planning</u>:

> "Financial planners typically provide advice on investments and consumer debt management. However, generally financial planners have been better trained to give investment advice than to give advice on mortgages. The reason for this maybe (1) the slant of most training for financial planners is toward providing investment advice or (2) planners and FSPs are most often employed by or earn their incomes through companies that distribute investments or financial products.

> For a commission only planner, the monies not applied toward the mortgage(s) may be viewed as monies available for making commissionable investments. A mortgage creates a gray area for the average financial planner because it's the largest consumer debt and yet it's tied to what may be or generally is the client's biggest physical asset (their home). In this instance, advice should not be given on the debt without considering the impact on the asset."

If you can't count on a financial planner to make you aware of the benefits of the imputed rental value and how it differs from the benefits of the mortgage interest deduction, whom can you count on?

NOTES:

The Need For
Mortgage Planning

"If you do it NOW, you've WON."
Jack Lalane

For years I've advocated the need for mortgage planning and have written several books on the subject: *Managing Your Mortgage To Financial Independence, The Book on Mortgage Planning, and The ABCs of Mortgage Based Financial Planning.* However, over the past few years, this term has been corrupted by people trying to sell a mortgage or investments so I must caution you that there are some who refer to themselves as "mortgage planners" when like some who refer to themselves as financial planners they are not actually planning professionals, but are using the "planning label" to convey knowledge, skills, abilities and experience they don't have. Mortgage planning, as I define it, is all about the mortgagor (you), mortgagor risk identification, risk classification, full disclosure, and control and management of mortgage related decisions.

As defined in *The Book on Mortgage Planning*:

> "Mortgage planning is a client focused goal oriented process of efficiently allocating and managing a mortgagor's resources and risks in a way that takes into account the mortgagor's lifestyle goals and objectives with due consideration given to the mortgagor's personality and socioeconomic environment to arrive at the most appropriate mortgage decision under the circumstances."

The Book on Mortgage Planning defines a mortgage planner as:

> "A professional that follows the mortgage planning process and recognizes the mortgage on a primary residence as part of a client's total portfolio and is capable, qualified and offers to provide mortgage planning services (actionable information) up to the evaluation level (the highest level on Bloom's Taxonomy) while maintaining high ethical standards by not promoting fraudulent or unethical mortgage practices."

Mortgage planners should all speak the same language and use that language when communicating with the consuming public that's why I developed the study of Mortgage Based Financial Planning™. Rather than making mortgage decisions in a vacuum, Mortgage Based Financial Planning™ (MBFP) focuses on assessing the suitability of an individual consumer's mortgage related decisions and on recognizing the potential short-term and long-term impacts of their decisions such that the practitioner can provide value added personalize mortgage advice. MBFP is not linked to the sale of any financial services products and it's intended to be fee-only services. The only compensation received is for the value of the services rendered.

As stated in *The ABCs of Mortgage Based Financial Planning*:

> "With over thirty years since the advent of financial planning and with over 100,000 financial planners, how can it be that the average consumer is faring worse than yesteryears? Why are personal savings at record lows? Why is home equity being used to keep consumers afloat? Why are some financial planners working with mortgage originators to encourage homeowners to tap into home equity to fund investment and insurance programs? Wouldn't you think it would be just the opposite? Wouldn't you think that overtime the profits from investments and insurance programs would be sufficient to pay off the mortgage?
>
> If after thirty years financial planning gets a failing grade, what alternatives are available that might work better for the consumer? Is there a better approach to preparing for financial independence? Can planning by focusing on the biggest debt and most valuable physical asset bring about much needed financial improvement? Can expanding the numbers of practitioners who acquire the knowledge to bring about this change make financial independence a reality for more people much sooner?"

Of course I think the answer to these last questions is yes.

To the chagrin of the folks that want to sell you financial products, Mortgage Based Financial Planning™ recognizes that achieving financial goals, including financial independence, doesn't necessarily require that you save or invest the vast majority of your income, wait to achieve a return on an investment, nor does it require you to assume any or any more investment risk than you already have.

MBFP is a course of study offered by the Mortgage Institute For Financial Services Professionals, Inc. (MIFSP). MIFSP supports the belief that the provision of financial planning services is a very valuable service unto itself and can be provided independent of any other product or service, and thus promotes the growth of fee-only services. The MIFSP program, whether taken as the workshop or a self-study course, combines some of the best practices in financial planning and mortgage analyzing techniques, with a client centered focus because traditional financial planning, in and of itself, may not result in capturing a plan that encompasses obtaining, monitoring and managing the mortgage or it may not result in accurately assessing the financial impacts of having a mortgage.

Through this MIFSP course, practitioners are shown how to detect the common mistakes made by consumers when making mortgage decisions, often with the help of well-meaning financial advisors, such as:

1)   Not realizing that mortgage decisions impact other financial goals and objectives;

2)   Ignoring known and anticipated new debts, expenses or expected reductions in income;

3)   Pulling equity out of the home for reasons other than financial hardship or making improvements that increase the value of the property;

4)   Not developing and implementing a financial plan that includes consideration of prepaying the mortgage;

5)   Over valuing the mortgage interest deduction and/or incorrectly calculating its value;

6)   Risking equity to make investments without acknowledging risk differentials or the additional mortgage payment that must be made while waiting for the investment to grow;

7)   Not recognizing the economic as well as accounting benefit of making sound mortgage decisions;

8)   Not realizing that the principle of leverage is often inappropriately applied to a primary residence;

9)   Not recognizing the tax-free rental value of a debt free home;

10) Not recognizing the basic equation for taxation;

11) Not recognizing the differences between a tax deduction, tax deferral, a tax exemption and a tax credit when it comes to the mortgage; and

12) Believing that equity in the home is an idle asset.

Often with the help of well-meaning financial advisers, in striving for wealth accumulation, consumers commonly bypass the opportunity to achieve financial independence by ignoring a low risk, low to no cost alternative to investing, which is prepaying the mortgage. As a result, rather than growing and protecting the store of wealth in a purchased or paid for home, you have been conditioned to devalue this form of wealth and to view it as a chest of gold to be opened and consumed.

One of the missions of MIFSP is to help the consumer to realize the multifaceted value of a mortgage-free home and of its implications for achieving financial independence.

WHAT MORTGAGE BASED FINANCIAL PLANNING™ CAN DO FOR YOU

You should always keep in mind that a good financial plan and investment strategy must have a solid foundation in order to be successful. A mountain of debt does not provide a solid foundation.

Even though the home is the greatest store of wealth for most consumers, in the push for the accumulation of wealth, the home is overlooked as a means to achieve financial independence because of a persistent failure to recognize the mortgaged home for the trichotomy it represents as an asset, liability and store of value, coupled with the fact that no independent financial counsel for mortgages existed for the benefit of consumers. Housing expenses represent such a significant portion of the average consumers' outflow of cash that just focusing on managing this aspect of the consumers' finances will do far more for far more people than we may presently realize.

Mortgage Based Financial Planning™ is used to help the consumer develop a defensive position to any investment portfolio because through the effective management of the mortgage, consumers can create a dependable foundation that can secure their financial future.

The MIFSP makes the point that while investments are generally built around expectations of future performance, mortgage planning is based on guaranteed and/or contracted performance.

When funds are directed toward early extinguishments of mortgage debt, the outcome is guaranteed and the savings are quantifiable. With Mortgage Based Financial Planning™ we can answer questions such as: How much less money would have to be earned if the mortgage has been eliminated? If the mortgage is retired early, how much money is guaranteed to be saved? How much money (earned income or investment income) would then be needed to cover other living expenses?

The standard dogma of investment advice is that consumers, if they can get a rate of return elsewhere higher than the debt rate of their mortgage, should make the investment rather than pay off their mortgage. Comparing investing to prepaying a mortgage is an imbalanced comparison with potentially disastrous results.

Paying off the mortgage is a risk-free endeavor that reduces the borrower's liability with certainty. Comparing a risk-free payment to expected equity returns disregards the risk differential of the two options. Given this risk differential, it would be imprudent to dispense investment advice based solely on this type comparison.

No one has yet been able to identify an investment with comparable risk that provides the same level of benefit at the same cost as prepaying the mortgage. As consumers become more aware of the imbalance of this comparison, investors in large numbers may likely seek legal recourse to the extent that these types of comparisons cause them financial harm.

A mortgage free home is an excellent hedge against inflation, a down turn in the investment market, and an unexpected loss of income. This defensive position is a solid backdrop to the lack of guarantees in the investment market.

The Need to Create A Hierarchy of Investing

In *Managing Your Mortgage To Financial Independence*, I quote Merrill Lynch's advice from 1959 as it appeared in the Houston Chronicle, "*A Matter of Some Concern*", which involved imprudent speculation that went on to say that "when men take risks they can't afford to carry, when they put at stake money that they can't afford to lose, they speculate imprudently. They court trouble...No man should buy stocks *unless* he can cover his living expenses comfortably, *unless* he has adequate insurance to protect his family and *unless* he has set aside funds to meet emergencies...'Investigate – Then Invest.' " as there are no real get rich quick schemes that actually work. I also used a concept that was used by a company I represented many years ago to demonstrate the hierarchy of financial instruments used for creating financial security. The concept was an illustration of a pyramid (triangle) which symbolizes building a sound financial foundation from the bottom up. The level of risk goes up as you ascend the triangle. The concept appeared in Medical Economics, April 30, 1984.

As I said in *Managing Your Mortgage To Financial Independence*:

"Being that the company I was associated with was an insurance company, it's not surprising that at the base of the pyramid was insurance. However, even now, I can agree that having adequate insurance is a good start. There is no denying the wonders of life insurance and the ability to almost instantly create with a stroke of a pen and a few pennies on the dollar an estate equal to or many times greater than the value of a home and mortgage combined.

Census data shows that the median household is composed of 2.3 people, therefore, it is logical that a plan should be developed that protects the family whether the consumer lives, dies or becomes disabled. In preparing for these possibilities, we can apply management, investment, economic, risk management and even common sense principles to help us determine where we should put our money for the time we need it to work for us in order to reach our goal of financial independence.

Along with a foundation of insurance (life, health, disability income insurance& long term care, etc.), the consumer needs to set aside an emergency fund large enough to satisfy three to six months of their regular monthly expenses. This fund provides some financial protection in case of prolonged illness or joblessness and it also satisfies concerns regarding liquidity. It may be best to earmark these funds by setting up a separate interest-bearing account."

In Mortgage Based Financial Planning™, assuming you have a mortgage, the second level of this triangle will include a plan to pay off the mortgage because the savings from prepaying a mortgage are guaranteed. With a paid for home, you've provided yourself another layer of insurance. You've reduced your need to continue earning at the same level, you're better able to weather any economic storm, and you're in position to enjoy the full benefits of the imputed rental value of your home.

Mortgage Based Financial Planning™ Should Be A Financial Planning Specialty

Major financial planning associations readily recognize common specialties or areas of practice such as: cash management & budgeting, retirement planning, tax planning, investment planning, estate planning, and insurance planning (insurance planning may be further differentiated by areas of life, disability, long-term care, health and property/casualty, education funding, etc.). Hopefully, you should realize by now that a Mortgage Based Financial Planning™ specialty is as necessary as any of these specialties and, more importantly, it impacts the success of each one of the others. The Mortgage Based Financial Planning™ process can be implemented along with or prior to any other financial planning concentration.

A mortgage based financial plan includes the creation of a Mortgage Mission Statement™ and a Mortgage Strategy and Investment Policy Statement™. The Mortgage Mission Statement™ describes the financial objectives of your mortgage and the rationale for the mortgage. While the Mortgage Strategy and Investment Policy Statement™ describes with specificity the tactics and methods to be employed to maximize the benefits of having a mortgage while simultaneously minimizing the total costs of having a mortgage. Writing these statements is a product of the Mortgage Optimization Theory™, which is one of two theories that are the underpinnings of Mortgage Based Financial Planning™.

The Mortgage Optimization Theory™ is based on the premise that the mortgage can be designed to maximize the benefits of having it while it's needed, to minimize the costs while it's in place, and to recognize when it's surpassed its optimal utility. MBFP empowers the consuming public, and those who guide them, to be cognizant of the suitability and applicability of various financial concepts (such as leverage, return on equity, annual returns, return after tax, wasted asset) and the risks associated with having a mortgage on a primary residence. The primary goal of this mortgage planning process is to encourage mortgagors to reconcile the risk and rewards associated with having, holding and disposing of a mortgage on their primary residence.

As recognized in *Managing Your Mortgage To Financial Independence*:

'The long-term nature of the mortgage tends to encourage a heavy reliance on the mortgage such that it can become a financial crutch. Consequently, consumers are sent wrong messages resulting in investing and spending habits that are counterproductive to achieving financial independence."

Given this observation, is it possible that by embracing Mortgage Based Financial Planning™ as a financial planning specialty we can do wonders to improve financial literacy and financial education, even beyond those efforts on the federal level?

Financial Literacy and Education on the Federal Level

"Insanity: doing the same thing over and over again and expecting different results."
Albert Einstein

T hroughout most of the previous decade and up until now, various commissions and councils have been created by acts of Congress or by Executive Order of the President with the stated charge of improving financial literacy among all Americans. Here are several examples. In 2003, Congress created the Financial Literacy and Education Commission ("FLEC") through passage of the Financial Literacy and Education Improvement Act under Title V of the Fair and Accurate Credit Transactions Act of 2003. This Commission was chaired by the Secretary of the U.S. Department of Treasury and was composed of 19 other agencies. The FLEC was to work with its member Federal agencies to improve financial literacy and education and provide free, reliable financial information to the American public.

I must stop here before moving on and say that the information provided by these agencies, and even the Commission itself, may have been free, but it wasn't always reliable. The head of the Department of Housing and Urban Development was one of the members of this Commission and a mortgage calculator found through the website of that agency was one of the faulty calculators identified in *The Red Report* as providing grossly exaggerated tax savings from mortgaging a home. It's ironic that HUD was contributing to financial illiteracy at the same time the head of the agency was sitting on this Commission. What's even more laughable is that the mortgage calculator consumers were directed to from the actual website of the Financial Literacy and Education Commission was also defective according to *The Red Report*. It's no wonder that even with the heads of all of these agencies working together and a newly formed literacy commission, Americans remained financially illiterate.

On January 22, 2008, President Bush signed an Executive Order creating, for the first time, a President's Advisory Council on Financial Literacy. The charge of this Council was simply to improve financial literacy among all Americans. The following was taken from the first Annual Report of this Council:

> "We believe the market turmoil and credit crisis of 2008 underscore the critical need for improved financial literacy in the United States. While there are many causes to the economic

problems facing the country, it is undeniable that a lack of financial literacy is a contributing factor. Far too many Americans entered into home and other loan agreements that they did not understand and ultimately could not afford. More broadly, the lack of basic skills such as how to create and maintain a budget, understand credit, or save for the future are preventing millions of Americans from taking advantage of our vibrant economic system. And tens of millions of our citizens are either unbanked or underserved, which leaves them outside the economic mainstream. Addressing these issues is critical to the future of our nation's economy."[8]

Let me quote again a portion of one of those lines above: "Far too many Americans entered into home and other loan agreements that they did not understand and ultimately could not afford." Faulty mortgage calculators probably induced many of these mortgages according to the information cited in *The Red Report*, but that wasn't mentioned in the Annual Report. Can you really blame financial illiteracy when homeowners rely on information that's been provided by trusted financial institutions and other financial advisors that they're suppose to be able to depend on? By the way, this Council was also created under the U.S. Department of Treasury, and according to *The Red Report*, at least one of its members is also affiliated with one of the companies that were found to have a faulty mortgage calculator. Is that irony or tragedy?

Most recently, President Obama created the President's Advisory Council on Financial Capability by Executive Order on January 29, 2010. This Council was also established within the Department of the Treasury. In addition to the Secretary of the Treasury and the Secretary of Education, the Council is to consist of not more than twenty-two

(22) members appointed by the President "from among individuals not employed by the Federal Government." Financial capability as defined in the Executive Order is the "capacity, based on knowledge, skills, and access, to manage financial resources effectively." The Executive Order goes on to say that "financial capability empowers individuals to make informed choices, avoid pitfalls, know where to go for help, and take other actions to improve their present and long-term financial well-being." On October 12, 2010, President Obama announced his twelve (12) intended appointments to this Council. The following was taken from a White House press release issued on that day.

> "The Council will provide advice to the President on promoting and enhancing financial literacy and capability among the American people. This effort is important to help keep America competitive and assist the American people in understanding and addressing financial matters, which contributes to our national financial stability. The Council has been tasked with a number of charges, including advising the President on: financial education efforts; promoting financial products and services that are beneficial to consumers, especially low- and moderate-income consumers; and promoting understanding of effective use of such products and services.
>
> The new Council is a part of President Obama's broader commitment to promote financial capability and protect American consumers. One of the central aspects of the Dodd-Frank Wall Street Reform and Consumer Protection Act that President Obama recently signed into law is the creation of the Consumer Financial Protection Bureau (CFPB), the sole mission of which is protect and empower American consumers with the clear and concise information they need to make the financial decisions that are best for them and their families. The CFPB will house a new Office of Financial Education that will help educate and empower consumers to make better informed financial decisions. The President's Advisory Council

on Financial Capability will play an important role in complementing these efforts. The President will announce additional members to this Committee at a later date."

Of the twelve members on this Council, two of them have ties to companies identified in *The Red Report* as having faulty mortgage calculators, and another member is Chairman and CEO of a nonprofit organization that just received a very fat check from one of the other companies identified in *The Red Report*. Again, is this irony or tragedy?

Maybe it's irony and tragedy. It's ironic that some of the same companies *The Red Report* identifies as having provided information that exploits the consumers' lack of financial knowledge are now sitting on the Council that's suppose to develop ways to close that knowledge gap, but it's also tragic that the consumers' hopes of learning how to avoid dire financial situations have been put in the hands of representatives from some of the very same companies that may have helped put them there.

Richard Ketchum, Chairman and CEO of the Financial Industry Regulatory Authority Inc. and a member of the Council was quoted in an article that appeared in "Investment News" as endorsing investment advice practitioners playing a role in the Council's financial literacy efforts. He identified investment advice practitioners as well as broker-dealers as being an important linchpin. That sounds like more irony and tragedy, and it creates another inherent conflict of interest being that there are no mandated disclosure requirements when dispensing financial advice on the home.

It should not go unnoticed that most of these practitioners have been indoctrinated in a sales culture (insurance & investments), the majority of them are not operating in a fiduciary capacity, and they are primarily paid by commission sales so the desire to educate may conflict with the will to sell. There are financial practitioners who are willing to work for free with the hopes of being paid on the sale of various products or services that a client or potential client would need in the execution of the plan provided. This means that they are working on a 100% commission basis. There are financial practitioners who work on a fee and commission basis. There are financial practitioners who work on a fee-offset basis (they charge a fee but credit any commissions received against the fee). There are also financial practitioners who claim to be fee-only, but who see no problem accepting fees based on a percentage of the amount of assets under management while believing that there is something inherently wrong with receiving commissions. It's no coincidence that the vast majority of Americans never speaks to, yet alone work with a financial planner on an ongoing or even an annual basis because most planners, as history and the empirical evidence indicates, have a financial product orientation instead of a proven consumer, customer or client orientation.

For these financial literacy programs to work, the educators need to be educated enough to do the educating. Case in point, there were (and may still be) many financial planners with extensive marketing programs promoting the idea of consumers borrowing home equity to purchase financial products, which as I previously mentioned, not only increases the mountain of mortgage debt, but also puts the homeowner at greater risk. Some of these marketing programs even appear to have had the support of the Financial Planning Association.

If you don't know, the financial planning industry regulates itself so why urge consumers to seek the services of financial planners when there's no consistency in what the consumer gets or in what they should even expect to get? Unfortunately, looking for financial planning credentials isn't always enough. Expecting these practitioners to be the linchpin for financial literacy is like letting the fox guard the hen house. And as a very wise man once said, if we keep doing the same thing over and over again, how can we expect a different result?

NOTES:

Shining a Light on the Biggest Mortgage Fraud of All

"A question that sometimes drives me hazy: am I or are the others crazy?"
Albert Einstein

How can it be that for years, decades even, the biggest mortgage fraud of all could have managed to continue to exist and then become one of the most exploited financial biases we may ever know? How is it that we were led to believe that the mortgage interest deduction was the greatest tax benefit of homeownership and possibly the only tax benefit of homeownership? How can it be that we rarely, if ever, hear any financial advisors promote the tax benefit that comes with a paid for home? How can it be that the only time the words "imputed rental value" are mentioned is when the Internal Revenue Service is looking for another source of taxable income?

How is it that we came to believe that equity in a home has a zero rate of return? How is it that we came to believe that one of the best ways to achieve financial wealth was to get the biggest fattest mortgage and keep it? How is it that we came to believe that a paid for home was undesirable? Well, undoubtedly, it took a lot of key players to pull this off among them we find banks, financial planners, financial brokers, and even some governmental entities.

As some believers drown in financial hardships, most of the survivors continue to believe in these very same ideas. How do we change the consumers' view of these misconceptions?

Frankly, until consumer ignorance becomes less profitable and until fewer heads look the other away when that ignorance is exploited, most likely not much is going to change. Even though financial literacy may be a stated goal of our society, financial illiteracy is extremely profitable for a lot of people.

How will the stated goal of financial literacy on a consumer level be balanced against the profitability of financial illiteracy on a business level?

Being that a mortgaged home represents a trichotomy of being an investment, a physical asset and a financial liability, about seven years ago, I formulated a couple of theories to help financial services practitioners enable their clients/homeowners to recognize the special position that a mortgage on the primary residence holds in relation to the assets in their client's financial portfolio. These theories were developed from the perspective that in helping a client achieve their core financial objectives, the practitioner should probably be concerned with reducing the level of debt obligations that have to be serviced from current cash flow. These two theories would do wonders to advance financial literacy and decrease the profitability of financial illiteracy, so you've probably heard even less about them than imputed rental value. These theories are the underpinnings of Mortgage Based Financial Planning™. In the previous unit, I mentioned one of the theories, the Mortgage Optimization Theory™. Below is a brief discussion of the other theory.

The Mortgage Portfolio Theory

The Mortgage Portfolio Theory (MPT) states:

> A mortgage free home is a defensive position in any portfolio, and because mortgage financing may be used as a means of financing more than just the acquisition or improvement of the associated property, homeowners may unwittingly take more risk, at far greater expense, and a much lower return than necessary in the pursuit of their financial goals, not realizing that prepaying the mortgage either systematically or in a lump sum should be viewed just as favorably as any investment in the portfolio, and the higher the percentage of income from salaries and wages that goes towards meeting housing expenses, the more significant the need to establish a defensive portfolio position and to properly define and assess comparable risk/return differentials.[9]

More simply stated, it means that the best defensive position in any investment portfolio, for a person who has a mortgage, is a plan to prepay the mortgage. Consequently, disclosure of the guaranteed return and no cost-no risk nature of prepaying the mortgage should be a self-imposed ethics obligation for any financial services professional that sells investments or investment advice. Most financial services professionals make inappropriate comparisons between prepaying the mortgage and investing.

It's very common for professionals to make improper risk comparisons, improper tax calculations, and/or to ignore the impacts of the source of funds being invested, not to mention failing to factor in the impact of the consumer's contractual obligation to pay the mortgage while waiting for expected investment returns. When consumers invest, more than likely, they are expecting that their investments will grow sufficiently to keep them securely in their homes. The performance of the investment portfolio isn't guaranteed, but the results of effectively managing your mortgage can be.

The MPT focuses on making the consumer an informed consumer, increasing their awareness, by combining financial planning and investment management techniques and applying them to the mortgage. The theory recognizes the general long-term position of a mortgage in the consumer's expanded portfolio structure, and thus acknowledges the need to manage and monitor the mortgage like all other components making up the portfolio.

While there is no government oversight, control or regulation on those delivering financial planning advice, the amount of information delivered or the quality of advice received, these two theories provide a mechanism to make consistent and more informed financial decisions regarding saving, spending, investing, insuring and planning. You will also come to realize why the source of your income is crucial in determining what is best for you. Putting these theories in action consists of a series of analyses that are performed to tailor make decisions on an individual level.

The Significance of Housing Expenses

	2007	2008	2009
Average Annual Expenditures	$49,638	$50,486	$49,067
Housing	$16,920	$17,109	$16,895
% of total	**34.09%**	**33.89%**	**34.43%**

Source: Consumer Expenditure Survey-2009, U.S. Department of Labor, Bureau of Labor Statistics, released 10/5/2010.

The Bureau of Labor Statistics Consumer Expenditure Survey data measures how consumers allocate their spending among the various components of total expenditures. It probably comes as no surprise that the single largest component of the consumers' budget has consistently been housing as indicated by the latest figures from the 2007 - 2009 Consumer Expenditure Survey, which shows housing expenses respectively averaged 34.09%, 33.89%, and 34.43% of gross income before taxes for all consumer units.

With over 30% of the average income going towards housing and 66% of all households being owner occupied households, it shouldn't be surprising that the largest single asset most Americans have is their home.

Legislators, regulators and others recognize that although people have been buying and dreaming of buying homes for years, there is still a deficiency in the knowledge of the average homebuyer that leaves them vulnerable. Consumers either learn by trial and error or they never learn that they erred at all. Housing expenses represent such a significant portion of the average consumers' outflow of cash that just focusing on managing this aspect of the consumers' finances will do far more for far more people than we may presently realize.

The Mortgage Portfolio Theory™ and the Mortgage Optimization Theory™ are designed to help Americans achieve financial independence. When I say financial independence it is not to be confused with wealth. You can achieve financial independence without being "wealthy". Wealth is relative. Financial independence can be defined on ones own terms and should be based on your ability to sustain your chosen lifestyle. Since Americans typically spend more on housing than any other expense, how much easier, financially, is it for those reaching retirement that are living in a mortgage-free home? Are they better prepared to live on less income?

So, can planning by focusing on the biggest debt and most valuable physical asset bring about much needed financial improvement? I think so.

How Do We Shine a Light on the Biggest Mortgage Fraud of All?

The answer to this question can be summed up in one word – disclosure – either self-imposed by industry or mandated by law.

What do you think would happen if there was required disclosure of the tax benefits of the imputed rental value any time a consumer is sold a mortgage or an investment of any kind? What if there was required disclosure that this tax benefit could far exceed the tax benefits of the mortgage interest deduction? What if there was required disclosure of how the imputed rental value impacts the mortgaged home as well as the home once it's fully paid for? What if there was required disclosure of the financial benefits of a paid for home in all financial plans offered by all financial planning experts and other financial services providers? What if your investment advisor had to disclose the minimum required yield, or hurdle rate, that an investment has to reach in order to meet the principal and interest payment on your home? What if your investment advisor was required to calculate and disclose an investment yield for the investor to use when making a comparison of mortgage prepayment options to investment alternatives?

Do you think this kind of disclosure would bust the MID myth, eliminate the MID bias, and reduce the kinds of mortgage fraud that exploits the consumers' financial bias towards the mortgage interest deduction, thereby encouraging consumers to take more risk than necessary and leading them to unknowingly over-consume, over-purchase, over-borrow, and over-mortgage their homes? Do you think this kind of disclosure would have a material impact on consumer mortgage and investment decisions? If you think so, shouldn't it be a required disclosure?

With disclosures like this, over time, the result would probably be fewer mortgage defaults, fewer foreclosures, fewer dislocated families, fewer dollars inappropriately at risk in the investment market, paid for homes serving as a defensive financial portfolio position, fewer dollars needed for retirement, less reliance on social security benefits, and more people again enjoying financial independence.

Score one for financial literacy.

Epilogue

As you now know, the biggest mortgage fraud of all involves acts and practices that, among other things, perpetuates the myth or otherwise encourages consumers to believe that the single largest tax benefit available to them annually as homeowners is the mortgage interest deduction.

This myth has so permeated our national housing, tax and financial culture that it has persisted for decades despite the fact we as Americans have many of the most advanced, educated, and regulated housing, tax and financial systems in the world.

While the myth has seemingly escaped the scrutiny of academia, legislators, regulators, and consumers it didn't escape commercial exploitation by thousands of banks and other financial services providers to the detriment of consumers, the housing, tax and financial marketplaces. I believe this myth has also been detrimental to the economy, competition, professional development, the acceptance and practice of personal financial planning, and the more specialized practice of mortgage planning.

Despite all that is reasonable, the existence, magnitude and persistence of this myth, bias and fraud is indicative of a specific failure, inability or unwillingness of the vast majority of American regulators, providers and consumers to distinguish between associated marketing material, financial education, financial fact and financial fiction.

I believe this myth, the bias and the fraud also indicates our persistent failure, inability or unwillingness to differentiate between those practitioners and providers who make us aware of material, decision-making information, those who claim to do so but don't, and those who don't even bother to make an effort to make us aware of anything of lasting value.

APPENDIX

Please Note:

Prior to the current appeal, I sent a letter and a complimentary copy of a publicly available research report entitled *The Red Report, When Banks Don't Compete – The Case of The Mortgage Calculator* to:

1. President, Barack Obama, April 15, 2009
2. Treasury Secretary Timothy F. Geithner, April 15, 2009
3. FTC Chairman Jon Leibowitz, April 15, 2009
4. FDIC Chairman Sheila Bair, April 15, 2009
5. HUD Secretary Shaun Donovan, April 15, 2009
6. Fed Chairman Ben S. Bernanke, April 15, 2009
7. OCC Comptroller John C. Dugan, April 15, 2009
8. OTS Director John M. Reich, April 15, 2009
9. NCUA Chairman Michael Fryzel, April 15, 2009
10. CFP Board CEO Kevin R. Keller, August 19, 2009
11. American College President Laurence Barton, August 26, '09
12. LIMRA/LOMA CEO Robert Kerzner, August 26, 2009
13. Ameriprise Financial CEO James Cracchiolo, August 26, '09

It is now over a year and half later and the American people are still trying to make intelligent, informed financial housing, tax and financial decisions, and unfortunately, they are still being subjected to unfair, deceptive and abusive banking practices that are not in the consumers, banks or our country's long-term best interests.

Exhibit A: Summary of The IRV vs. MID

		Imputed Rental Value	Mortgage Interest Deduction
1	Tax benefit available to all homeowners	Yes	No
2	Tax benefit available annually	Yes	Yes
3	Tax Deduction	No	Yes
4	Tax Exemption	Yes	No
5	One Time Tax Credit	No	No
6	Homeowner must sign an instrument	No	Yes
7	Home must be security for debt in case of default	No	Yes
8	Mortgage/Deed Instrument must be recorded	No	Yes
9	Requires that home be a Qualified Home	No	Yes
10	Home acquisition debt limitations	No	Yes
11	Home equity debt limitations	No	Yes
12	Tax benefit available with a reverse mortgage	Yes	No
13	Tax benefit varies depending on year debt acquired	No	Yes
14	Modified Adjusted Gross Income Limitations	No	Yes
15	Homeowner must be ready to substantiate all values used	No	Yes
16	Requires Filing IRS Long Form 1040	No	Yes
17	Requires Filing A Federal Tax Schedule	No	Yes
18	Internal Revenue Service (IRS) Can Audit the Amounts*	No	Yes
19	Internal Revenue Service (IRS) Can Adjust The Amounts*	No	Yes
20	Taxpayer may lease the home	Yes	No
21	Taxpayer can acquire the home by gift	Yes	Yes
22	Taxpayer can acquire the home by inheritance	Yes	Yes
23	Taxpayer can acquire the home from a related person	Yes	Yes
24	Taxpayer must purchase home by specified date	No	No
25	Home Financing Source Irrelevant (Tax-Free M.R. Bonds)	Yes	No
26	Taxpayer can sell the home at any time	Yes	Yes

* The IRS can adjust the amount if taxpayer is a tenant renting/leasing the home.

Quick Survey Check
To Test Your Awareness Of The Biggest Mortgage Fraud of All
Please Indicate Your Preference
Between
The MID & The Imputed Rental Value (IRV)

Note: For each characteristic identified, please indicate your preference in the right hand column.

Characteristic or Featured Benefit	Tax Benefit #1 MID	Tax Benefit #2 IRV	Your Preference/ # 1 or #2.
Requires Itemization on Tax Return (1040)	Yes	No	
Requires Itemized Deductions to exceed Standard Deduction	Yes	No	
Requires Debt	Yes	No	
Requires Qualified Debt	Yes	No	
Encourages Home Equity Debt	Yes	No	
Maximum Qualified Debt	$1,000,0000	Unlimited	
Maximum Home Equity Debt	$100,000	Unlimited	
Encourages Home Ownership	Yes	Yes	
Available with No Mortgage	No	Yes	
Available with a Reverse Mortgage	No	Yes	
Deduction	Yes	No	
Exclusion	No	Yes	
Encourage MPT*	Yes	Yes	N/A
Encourage MOTH**	Yes	Yes	N/A

Total times you selected #1 _____ & #2 _____

---

1. Are the MID and the IRV benefits mutually exclusive?

2. Do you have enough information to make an informed choice between these two benefits?

3. Do you need more information so that you can make an intelligent and informed decision about these two benefits?

Given the above relatively brief comparison of the two tax benefits:

4. Did your reliance on the MID influence your decision to obtain either a first or second mortgage?

5. Would you have obtained a mortgage or the same size mortgage if you knew that the MID was not going to provide the tax savings you were lead to believe it would?

6. Were you counting on the tax savings from the MID to make the mortgage/housing costs more affordable?

7. If you pulled equity out of your house by obtaining a bigger mortgage or a home equity line of credit (HELOC), would you have obtained the same size mortgage or HELOC if you knew that it would not result in greater tax savings through the MID?

8. Were you counting on the tax savings from the MID on a larger mortgage/HELOC to make a larger mortgage/house more affordable?

9. Would you have obtained a mortgage/bigger mortgage if the mortgage calculator you used more accurately reflected the tax savings from the MID?

10. If the mortgage calculator you used properly reflected the tax savings from the MID, would you have obtained the same size mortgage any way?

11. Would you have obtained a mortgage or the same size mortgage if you had been made aware of the benefits of the IRV?

12. If you currently have or have ever had a mortgage, would you have made different investment decisions if you had been made aware of the benefits of the IRV?

About The Author

Leon L. Morris, CLU, ACS, ChFC, CME, ALMI, FFSI
Residential Mortgage Planner, RMP®

Leon Morris started his financial services career in 1983 as an insurance agent in Florida. Since then, Leon has worked in the insurance and financial services industry as a Special Agent, Sales Manager, Personally Producing General Agent, Registered Representative, Mortgage Broker and Registered Investment Adviser. Leon also worked for a number of years as a Senior Associate (Technical Specialist & Product Manager) for the Life Office Management Association (LOMA). During his employment with LOMA, Leon was directly responsible for product development in the Association's Management Resources Division with a focus on equity products, annuities, broker-dealer operations and pensions.

Leon was engaged in original research, creating, organizing, promoting and conducting technical training seminars and workshops, and managing executive level committee meetings throughout the United States and Canada. Leon has been President & CEO of Morris Capital Management (MCM) since he founded the company in June of 1995. MCM has operated as a Georgia Residential Mortgage Licensee, a Florida Licensed Mortgage Brokerage Business, and a Registered Investment Adviser. Leon is the Executive Director of the Mortgage Institute for Financial Services Professionals, Inc. (MIFSP).

Leon completed his under graduate degree with an interdisciplinary double major concentration in economics and government from the College of Social Sciences at Florida State University in 1985. He received designations as a Chartered Life Underwriter (CLU) and Chartered Financial Consultant (ChFC) from the American College in 1991 and 1993, respectively. Leon received the Associate, Customer Service (ACS) designation from LOMA with honors in the first class of designees in 1992 and LOMA's Fellow, Financial Services Institute (FFSI) in 2005. He was also awarded LOMA's Associate, Life Management Institute (ALMI) in 2006. Leon received the Certified Mortgage Evaluator (CME) designation and Residential Mortgage Planner, RMP® designation in 2003 from the Mortgage Institute for Financial Services Professionals, Inc. (MIFSP).

Leon has held the National Association of Securities Dealers (NASD) now known as the Financial Industry Regulatory Authority (FINRA) Series 6, 7, and North American Securities Administrators (NASA) Series 63, and 65. He has held Georgia licenses for life, health and variable products. He has also held a Florida and Georgia mortgage broker's license. Leon is author of the books *Managing Your Mortgage To Financial Independence*, *You Don't Have To Chase Wealth to Achieve Financial Independence; The ABCs of Mortgaged Based Financial Planning; The Book on Mortgage Planning;* and *The Red Report, When Banks Don't Compete – The Case of The Mortgage Calculator.* Leon currently resides in the metro Atlanta area with his wife of twenty-six years and their two teenage children.

End Notes

[1] MYFSP™ C3 Exam

[2] www.IRS.gov (154,396K/39,199K) Table#2 &2.2

[3] The Red Report, When Banks Don't Compete - Page 37.

[4] $2,048,546,621 individual v. total $2,345,337,177 or 87% Source: IRS 2009 Data book.

[5] 80/20 principle.

[6]
www.boston.com/news/education/higher/galleries/061110 housing and pay of college pr
esidnts/ *What they make, and where they live* & 2nd article: *Light shed on housing for college Presidents*

[7] http://www.financial-planning.com/news/financial-planning-coalition-2661689-
1.html?zkPrintable=true FPA magazine 4-2009

[8] First Annual Report of the President's Advisory Council on Financial Literacy, page 8

[9] *The ABC's of Mortgaged Based Financial Planning*, January 2005

www.ingramcontent.com/pod-product-compliance
Lightning Source LLC
Chambersburg PA
CBHW071840200326
41519CB00016B/4185